TO ANGER, With Love

TO ANGER,
With Love

Elizabeth R. Skoglund

1817

HARPER & ROW, PUBLISHERS
New York, Hagerstown, San Francisco, London

Grateful acknowledgment is made to the following for permission to reprint selections included in this book:

HARPER & ROW, PUBLISHERS, INC. for quotations from *Guilt and Grace* by Paul Tournier. Copyright © 1958 by Delachaux and Niestle S.A. English translation copyright © 1962 by Hodder & Stoughton, Ltd. Reprinted by permission of Harper & Row, Publishers, Inc.

W.W. NORTON & COMPANY, INC. for a selection from "The Man Who Was Put in a Cage" in *Man's Search For Himself* by Rollo May Ph.D. Copyright 1953 by W.W. Norton & Company, Inc., New York, N.Y.

FIRST EDITION

Designed by Eve Callahan

Library of Congress Cataloging in Publication Data

Skoglund, Elizabeth.
　To anger, with love.
　Includes bibliographical references.
　1. Anger. I. Title.
BF575.A5S5 1977　　152.4　　76–62937
ISBN 0–06–067392–3

152.4
S628

77 78 79 80 81 10 9 8 7 6 5 4 3 2 1

Contents

Preface   7

Foreword by Paul Tournier   9

1. It's Okay to be Angry   13
2. When Christians Are Angry   24
3. Childhood Anger   35
4. Using Anger in Relationships   49
5. A Bad Day at Work   65
6. Stored-Up Anger: Depression   75
7. Creative Anger   95

To those who have felt deeply life's pain and its subsequent anger and then have been forced to endure a barrage of well-meant but misguided criticism from those who should understand, this book is dedicated in the hope that they will find in it a relief from guilt and will gain a usefulness in the anger which up to now has been misunderstood and misused.

Preface

Anger in its harshest form of expression is splashed daily across our newspaper headlines in the announcement of violent crimes. Due to the television media we are the first generation to have witnessed personally a presidential assassination. In our fear of violence many of us engage in debates on gun control while others quietly buy attack dogs or burglar alarm systems to protect what seems in jeopardy.

Anger is a problem in twentieth century American living. Yet that same anger which seethes inside and produces psychosomatic illnesses in some and in others precipitates acts of violence can at the same time by some people be safely ventilated and channelled constructively. I see anger graphically in its most negative as well as positive forms. I observe the ruined marriages which have been slowly eroded away by caustic remarks and small acts of anger. I hear the anger of the teenage delinquent, lashing at "society" while he continues his crimes of small thefts and gang violence in a futile, self defeating effort to release a deep burning sense of resentment.

Positively, however, I see young people survive and overcome unbelievable obstacles in order to accomplish what they want in life and in many cases an anger which literally said "I will not be destroyed" motivated them successfully. The same can be said of people at various ages, with vastly differing problems. There are the aged who, angry at a life style for which they are largely denigrated stubbornly refuse to give in and so keep going instead. Then there are the vast majority of us who in many small ways either succumb to anger and become defeated and resentful or use our frustrations and even rage as an impetus for growth.

Anger can be positive. It can create growth. It does not need to destroy or even damage us. *To Anger, With Love* helps show the positiveness and the how-to of its creative potential. We would all prefer to never feel the pain of anger. But we live in a world where that option is nonexistant. For those who read this book there is the possibility of turning anger into something helpful and realizing that anger need be neither sinful nor destructive.

Once again as I have completed this manuscript I am grateful for the competent criticism of Glenn K. Wiest, Anne H. Pedrick, W. Roberts Pedrick, Marilyn Pendleton and my mother. I am indebted to Janet Camp for her efficient and patient typing of the manuscript. Not least, by far, my appreciation is extended to my editor, Marie Cantlon, for her positiveness and constructive advice.

Foreword

Anger!

Here we have a theme all too rarely approached with frankness, in spite of the important role it plays in daily life. Disputes occur frequently between husbands and wives (even those who love each other!), between brothers and sisters, between friends —to say nothing of all of the conflicts that arise on a social and international level. Anger constantly erupts everywhere, in spite of the universal condemnation with which it is greeted in refined circles. The person who seems the most reasonable can suddenly lose control and behave offensively. Often, one excuses oneself by referring precisely *to* the emotion: "Forget what I said—I was angry."

When the person tries to excuse him or herself, it is certainly because of feeling guilty over behaving in a manner contrary to ideals because of an unacceptable aspect of self. If anger emerges, it is because it was already present—latent, contained, but very real. Psychologists easily detect the blind, unexpressed anger hidden within all of us, even those who best know how to control themselves—those whom education and social pressure have trained in the art of repression.

Wouldn't it be better therefore to admit to oneself that anger is natural, that it is a part not only of the human condition, but of that of animals as well; it is inherent in the life process? Even God reveals himself to Moses as "quick to anger." In this way the Jewish scholar-philosopher Martin Buber formulates the Old Testament phrase, which he says "has furnished material for so many arguments," and which is generally translated by the less vivid "a jealous God" (Exod. 20:5).

Martin Buber informs us that the Hebrew word used there is old enough to be attributed to Moses himself, and that although it can certainly mean "jealous in the ordinary sense," it frequently "designates zeal for combat." Thus we are referring not merely to a state of mind, but to aggressive behavior. And that agrees well with the biblical record as a whole. The God of the Bible is not an immutable, impassive God, but a person —a living passionate God who acts and struggles.

Jesus himself beyond all doubt felt anger. The philosopher Karl Jaspers writes, "The Gospel shows us Jesus as an elemental force in his harshness and his aggressiveness, no less clearly than in other traits of infinite gentleness." Jesus has a spontaneity which contrasts sharply with our conventional attitudes. From where, then, does the guilt attached to anger come? Certainly not from the Bible, but from social pressure, which requires us to observe convention.

What the Bible forcefully denounces is hypocrisy. And there is a great deal of hypocrisy in the ideal of self-mastery, which is instilled in us from childhood on and becomes the source of serious forms of repression. The ideal is a Stoic and not at all a Christian one. Frequently, for example, one might see a woman having an attack of nerves while her husband stands by immobile, priding himself on the great "virtue" of his impassivity. And usually, his very insensitivity has caused his wife's anger—her only resource has been to explode into anger to force him into an understanding which he resists.

Thus anger is always the sign of a problem, and of a problem which one resists facing. The problem exists for the person who becomes angry as well as for the person who remains calm, carefully hiding his or her own anger while severely judging that of the other.

Here is a book which will make us think. We must all struggle to overcome our formidable resistance to recognizing ourselves as we are. The problems we can solve are those of which we allow ourselves to become aware. Elizabeth Skoglund can aid us in that task because her book is concrete, because it comes out of her extensive experience as a psychologist. But even more because she does not simply present us with cases to be submitted to a cold technical analysis, but because one can feel the warmth of her love for people—for children, for the aged, and for us, her readers, to whom she gives of herself generously . We all stand in need of a great deal of love in order to be able to accept ourselves as we really are.

Paul Tournier

Geneva, Switzerland
February 1977

1

It's Okay to be Angry

Laura stood in the middle of her lavishly furnished living room and stared numbly into the fireplace. Twenty minutes earlier her husband, Chuck, had walked out after what had been for him days of careful planning and preparation. For Laura there had been no warning. A last-minute goodbye and a closing of the front door sounded the finale to the major part of Laura's life. After twenty-five years, two children, and struggling to build a business—now this as an ending?

Suddenly Laura no longer felt numb. Instead she experienced a frightening rage, anger she had never known before. Without much thought she picked up an antique crystal vase that Chuck's mother had been given her. With cool control she aimed the family heirloom at the fireplace and threw it. The sound of tiny pieces of glass shattering against bricks was delightful, and the destructiveness of what she had done, right or wrong, somehow calmed Laura, and her rage diminished.

With a tight jaw and firmly pressed lips Jill slammed the front door of her mother's house and walked briskly to the car. A newlywed of about six months, Jill kept thinking, hoping she could visit her mother and talk out some of her problems. But it didn't work that way. Statements like "Well, I told you not to marry him in the first place" and "At least don't give him sex —and above all don't have children" had at last convinced Jill that her mother really wasn't going to change. As a child and as a teenager Jill had been turned off by the attitudes that sort of advice exhibited. Now that she was an adult, her reactions had not changed—she gritted her teeth and determinedly repressed her anger.

Anger is a common emotion, but at different times different people handle this potentially constructive or destructive feeling in different ways. While anger is considered a basically negative emotion, it is very possible to turn it into a positive, driving force for growth. We can determine whether we use anger positively or negatively, but we cannot decide to avoid feeling angry.

Infants exhibit anger before they are able to comprehend the world in which they live. Older children too frequently experience anger but are unsure of the boundaries within which that anger can be manifested.

Michael, a seven-year-old boy brought to me for counseling, slowly began to tell about his fears of dreams in which "bad men" broke into his room and hurt him. Bright, interesting, even affectionate, Mike was also afraid of people not liking him at school. Yet underneath was a seething rage directed at a world understandably irritated with this hyperactive child who could be a real handful in a group.

Finally Michael picked up a cushioned hammer in my toy room and with glee began mercilessly to beat a large inflated plastic clown. The clown's smile did not wither under the blows, and the happy look on Michael's face increased. At last out of sheer exhaustion Michael stopped, looked at me seriously, and asked, "Do I *really* get to come back here?" The question was more than an inquiry; it was a plea for help. At last Michael could safely and appropriately express anger without losing someone's approval or being rejected.

Although everyone occasionally feels anger, many people are even threatened by the thought that they are angry. When I told one man, "You are a very angry person," he shouted back, "I am *not* angry!"

Much entertainment attests to our need to indirectly release anger. TV violence is a classic, controversial example. We write, speak, and in general complain about violence on the tube in our living room, but do we really object? After all, the entertainment world, including television, pretty much gives us what we will watch, and apparently most people will watch violence. The why of this as well as the benefit or harm requires careful consideration.

In a thought-provoking editorial in *TV Guide*, John P. Roche commented on the pros and cons of TV violence:

> If you see a play in which a man murders his mother-in-law, is it more, or less, likely that you will go home and get an ax? Plato felt it would stimulate you to give the old girl a whack, and therefore banned drama and Homeric sagas from his Republic. Aristotle, in contrast, thought that watching the event on the stage was a form of therapy (catharsis he called it) and you would leave the theater purged of your murderous drives.[1]

I am inclined to agree with Aristotle although children and people with specific types of emotional disturbances might be exceptions. According to an article in a popular magazine, "more than 50 studies involving 10,000 children between the ages of three and nineteen have shown that the more violence and aggression a child watches on TV, the more likely he is to be violent and aggressive himself."[2] I believe such studies would have to be interpreted in light of many outside considerations such as the original emotional health of the children and the other anger-inducing factors in their lives.

And by the way, what happened to all of us who weren't raised on TV? As a child nothing freaked me out as much as the story of Bluebeard's grisly butchering of numerous wives. I heard it for the first time at a birthday party and was scared for days, but I didn't become aggressive because of it. And what about all the fairy tales that contained violence—little girls visiting their grandmothers who turned out to be wolves in disguise, giants almost catching little boys who were just trying to help poor mothers, children being chased out of their homes by a cruel stepmother only to be caught by a witch who tried to fatten and cook them? Somehow most of us remained unscarred from these episodes. We didn't think in terms of pathology or sick violence in those days. We just crawled deeper into the safe warmth of a soft quilt and enjoyed the deliciously scary stories which were read to us—and then sometimes asked for a night light!

As for people who already are deeply disturbed, Roche has a point when he says: " . . . it does not seem reasonable to me to design programming with him in mind. . . . most TV watchers are not lunatics."[3]

So much TV violence probably indicates that quietly, sometimes without confessing it to anyone, most of us at times sneak home after a frustrating, pressured day with just a little anger lurking in our personalities and conveniently, vicariously rid ourselves of it in front of the boob-tube.

Roche echoes our thoughts when he says:

> . . . I confess that I enjoy certain kinds of violent programs. *Gunsmoke,* for example, has kept me from going off the bridge on several tense occasions. To go home from the White House worrying about whether the world was going to end the day after tomorrow and turn on *Gunsmoke* was like getting my batteries recharged. You always knew, no matter how dicey things got, that in the end Matt Dillon would get his man, Good would triumph over Evil.
> Now that Matt is turning in his badge, I'll have to depend on *Cannon* and *Hawaii Five-O* for my therapy. In contrast, I dislike programs in which violence seems to be an end in itself, where it is extraneous to the plot and is obviously thrown in for sadistic kicks.[4]

And for those who stoutly deny the existence of such an anger and need for release, what about violent sports—football, boxing, motorcycle racing, judo? For some, these are both the evidence and the outlet for anger.

What about the businessman who works out with his punching bag or the executive dart board? Or the housewife who scrubs everything twice as hard when she's uptight? Or worst of all, the millions of bottled-up people who walk around developing peptic ulcers or preparing themselves for a coronary at fifty?

How can one explain the frantic anger of a California freeway? Try to change lanes when you've almost missed an off-ramp. Attempt to pass the person ahead of you who then promptly speeds up. Slow down just a little bit so you can read the signs before they flash by and listen to the horns begin to blare. A freeway is a battlefield of tired, often angry people taking out their feelings on other people who have never hurt them or even met them.

Nor are Christians exempt from the anger that seems to pervade the American scene. When I suggested to a pleasant, genuinely Christian woman that her relationship to Christ could be a help in her marital problems, she flashed back "Don't *you* tell me that. That's all I've heard from everyone else." She is deeply angry, perhaps even at God, but she's far from ready to see anger as the problem. Nor, I'm sure, would she go home and watch "Hawaii Five-O"! She's more likely to grow slowly bitter or to fight more with her husband or to internalize her feelings into a physical illness unless someone can show her that anger is not necessarily wrong and help her get the anger out in a responsible way and, better still, to use it as a handle for growth.

While anger has always characterized humankind, our society seems to have more than its share. Finding reasons for this is the first step in discovering how to handle and use anger.

Frustration and anger are closely related, and the rapid change of values in our society has contributed to a general sense of frustration. People seem unsure of who they are and what they should be doing. Even when they seem right, they feel wrong. A very bright woman said to me recently, "I am going to become a waitress [which meant leaving a well-paying job as a legal secretary] because my husband is threatened by my financial independence." A man who literally pushed his wife into working now blames her for not spending more time with her baby. A woman who expected faithfulness from her husband wanted to be sophisticated; so she got involved in mate swapping. Then she filed for divorce because her husband tried it! A medical doctor once said to me: "I'm not the success my colleagues are. They're specialists and I'm only in general practice." Yet his skill and certainly his relationships with patients far surpass those of many of his doctor-friends.

This confusion over male-female roles, moral ethics, success and its definition, and double standards generates anger in people. Christians too are caught up in the dilemma, but there are stabilizing factors. Christianity pretty well defines moral standards and success. Ethical problems can be worked out within a biblical framework. In the area of success, for example, the Bible clearly teaches that while what a person *does* is important, it is what one *is* inside that really counts. In counseling Samuel on his choice between the outwardly attractive Saul and the less flashy David, God said of Saul: "Look not on his countenance, or on the height of his stature; because I have refused him: for the Lord seeth not as man seeth; for man looketh on the outward appearance, but the Lord looketh on the heart" (1 Sam. 16:7). Such is God's definition of the highest form of success. According to it, the person who "fails" while giving his or her best succeeds far more in God's eyes than one who never tries and in some ways more than the person who succeeds with little effort. God puts a great premium on the inner life. Christians who really tune in to this will be disappointed but not destroyed and bitter over outward failure; and furthermore they will probably enjoy their successes but will not become haughty.

Although as Christians we can find spiritual resolutions for value changes, we can hardly avoid being affected by some of what's happening around us. Two most rapidly changing areas, for example, are marriage and sex. Wives are not sure what their roles really are nor do many husbands feel secure in their roles. If a woman works, how much of a homemaker does the man become? Are gentleness and aggressiveness female and male characteristics, respectively, or can a man be truly gentle and a woman aggressive without either feeling threatened?

Since divorce is accepted in our society as an almost norm, it is difficult to interpret the biblical view without unwarranted cultural distortions.

In all these issues it's hard not to go to extremes, for the balance requires thinking and even agonizing while extremes feel safe and comfortable—at least at the time. For example, a woman I know claims to be a Christian and yet has an active sex life with a variety of men. She experiences some conflict but not as much as might be expected because she has gone to an extreme of refusing to feel that God should have anything to say about what she does sexually. And she's not as unusual in that viewpoint as one might suppose.

At the other extreme is the woman who represses almost all sexual feelings and thus absolves herself of the conflict between balance and decision making.

Christians who grow but who also experience frustration and anger are those who feel, think, look around them, and then resolve their value problems in a manner that is both biblically and psychologically sound. At that point of balance the Christian can feel less frustrated over values than will the average thinking person. Nevertheless the Christian's position is often won only through stress.

Besides the frustration and anger created by fluctuating social values many people also experience inner hostility that is derived from a sense of rootlessness. This is partially the result of value conflict, but it is also due to the increased isolation of the individual in our society (and this affects Christians too). We buy services rather than act as friends. We pay for companions, baby-sitters, and transportation. We even pay for someone to listen to us. We don't take care of the elderly even when we can provide that care conveniently and without destroying our personal lives or our family's well-being. We shunt the aging off to institutions. We simply don't want to be involved, and so we feel lonely and again angry because pain always brings anger. Rather than change we buy antiques—even fake antiques!—to remind us that we have roots, and we look at "Little House on the Prairie" to remember that people care.

For Christians one of the basics is that we *do* love one another and that God loves us. As one little girl said, "Mother, we're related to those new people, aren't we?" Confused, her mother answered no. Upon which the child replied, "But I thought Christians were all part of the family of God!" Simple? Profound? Both. But even though we *know* this, we often look around us and *feel* the isolation and the anger, for isolation is painful and creates angry feelings. Sometimes we forget to *act* as we *believe.*

A woman who more than most people cares about people and extends herself was standing in line at a supermarket. It was midafternoon, and there were not many people in the store. She and the store manager chatted about pleasant trivia while she showed him a new ring her husband had just bought her.

Suddenly, not five feet ahead of her, a man dropped to the ground. He reminded her a little of her father: tall, graying at the temples, distinguished. She stood frozen, unable to act. The store manager called the paramedics while the man lay still, the color draining from his face.

Marlene knew how to do mouth-to-mouth resuscitation, but all she could think of was a lawsuit if she failed. Maybe someone else would do something.

Someone on the loudspeaker said, "Is there a doctor in the house?" No answer. "Is there a nurse?" No response. Finally, "Does anyone have any Red Cross training?" "I do," thought Marlene. "But, no, someone else will come—I might get sued —maybe he's okay. He doesn't look okay."

Then the sirens, the paramedics, the equipment, oxygen—but he was already dead. Would he have lived with earlier help? Maybe, maybe not. Marlene will never know, and she will never accept that she, a Christian, stood and watched a man die. She will never understand how, for that brief moment, she blended into a position of noninvolvement, but the fact that she did created mental pain and anger at herself for her temporary isolation in a society that more and more wants to be safe in its isolation. Involvement costs; noninvolvement, however, creates an emptiness and hostility that are much harder to handle.

Perhaps a feeling of meaninglessness is related to all the reasons for anger in our society. An increasing number of people seek psychological help because they are bored. Many of the very young feel an apathy toward life that promotes feelings of hostility as well as destructive behavior. Some teenagers claim they get loaded out of sheer boredom. True or not, that's how they feel. For all these people, weekends are harder to cope with than weekdays when their lives are more structured. In a way they both welcome and resent school and work. Extremes of individualism contribute to boredom because meaning can be found in relationships. Value changes and rootlessness make a person wonder what life is all about, and even the Christian, who is sure of his or her eternal destiny, may question the how and why of now.

For those who have low self-esteem and tend to devalue themselves, all general problems which generate anger become greatly intensified.

A middle-aged woman recently died of cancer. As I read the notice in the paper, I felt a mingled sense of relief for her and yet loss for what she could have done with her life. In our brief, rather distant encounter I found her to have all the ingredients which build toward a seething, bitter anger that destroys a person inside.

Everyone who knew her recognized her ambivalence toward life—a fight to live and a desire to die. She knew Christ, and that relationship was the only true love she could begin to grasp. She needed human love too and tried to find it in the beds of men who knew nothing of love, at least for her. Although it was difficult for her to accept *any* love because of her low self-image, she felt keenly the humiliation and anger of rejection. She saw herself as a giant zero on this earth, but she wanted to be a real person. Yet when someone tried to help her, she rejected the overture in deep anger as though involvement was more risky than the lonely pit of isolation she repeatedly chose. She tried suicide and then begged God to let her live. In a way she was almost a caricature of our society, an illustration in the extreme. She was lonely, unmotivated, bored, rootless, confused over values, and profoundly angry.

A young businessman walked into my office and said: "I must be angry. It's so buried, I don't even feel it, but I've left church and feel I need it. All I do is work. My marriage is a disaster, and I'm torn between my wife and just getting free and having uninvolved relationships with several women."

Presumably, he has a long life ahead of him. His anger will either cause him to react emotionally and behave irresponsibly —thus increasing his anger—or it will become a positive force in rebuilding his life. In one way or another, the same is probably true of many people in this world.

When I saw *The Hiding Place*, I had a mixed reactions. The movie as well as the book portrays a Dutch family interred in Nazi prison camps because they hid Jews. The story of the concentration camp focuses on two sisters, Betsy and Corrie ten Boom. While I was deeply challenged and in a way uplifted by the saintliness of Betsy who showed little anger and was portrayed as a positive force throughout the camp, Corrie seemed more real. She was angry. In a way, Betsy's saintliness depressed me because I don't feel that saintly. Corrie seemed more human without anything detrimental in the way of Christian testimony. She felt, she was angry, and perhaps the anger helped her get through the camp alive.

Christians are sometimes taught that anger is wrong. Even non-Christians view anger as a fault, a failing, a deficiency; yet anger is a normal reaction to pain. If you stub your toe, you feel pain—and anger. Anger is a warning to do something, a motivating force to get rid of pain. Anger, like many other emotions, can be abused or used. Perhaps therein lies its wrongness or rightness.

NOTES

1. John P. Roche, "Praise for Networks That Keep Gory Scenes off the Air," *TV Guide*, August 9–15, 1975, p. A–5.

2. Edwin Kiester, Jr., "TV Violence: What Can Parents Do?" *Better Homes and Gardens*, September 1975, p. 4.

3. Roche, *TV Guide*, p. A–6.

4. Ibid.

2

When Christians Are Angry

As the cigarettes piled up in the ash tray at his side, Mel Simpson, a successful business executive, became increasingly intense. His voice was loud; yet his words, rushing out quickly, were tightly controlled as if he were afraid the rage building up inside him might show or even become uncontrollable.

"In spite of all the pressure, I'm handling my problems quite well," he commented tersely. "After all, I haven't *once* lost my temper, and I don't feel I'm all that angry."

As I looked at his tight facial expression and watched the force with which he dug his cigarettes almost into oblivion in the ash tray, I wondered why this adequate, successful man could not admit he was truly very angry.

Haim Ginott offered an interesting comment relating to the view that contemporary society holds regarding anger:

> I once asked a group of 500 teachers if they remembered any lecturer in teachers college who said that children will often irritate them and make them angry and then told them how they could handle their anger constructively.
>
> None of the teachers had had such instruction.
>
> One teacher replied: "The fact that no one acknowledged

the problem told us a great deal. It told us that a good teacher never gets angry."[1]

Built into the framework of our society is the attitude that something is amiss when people feel anger. Children are told more often *not* to be angry rather than *how* to handle anger. Women are expected to suppress anger more than men because to show anger is not ladylike, just as men are expected to hide grief and tears. At the same time we are a violent society. Perhaps there is a causative relationship between those two facts, for when people hold in their anger too long, it becomes suppressed rage and can burst into violence.

I casually said to a man in the presence of his church-oriented wife, "You seem to be a rather angry person." Eagerly, as though it were a relief to admit this, he nodded yes. Immediately his wife contradicted him: "That's ridiculous, Sam. You're not at all angry."

Melissa, seven-year-old who was brought up in a strict Christian home, asked me cautiously, "Did you ever hate your friends at school when you were little?" I explained that I could remember many specific incidents when I had felt that way. She breathed a long sigh of relief and said, "Sometimes I hate my next-door neighbor." But the fear she showed as she built up to the subject and the time it took her to gather sufficient courage to ask the question again illustrates the stigma of anger in this society.

Parents, in particular, often exhibit real hesitancy in expressing anger about their children, at least to the outside world. Many children who feel great anger toward their parents express deep guilt feelings over that anger. While most people *feel* anger, many feel threatened by the acknowledgment of it.

Much of our attitude toward anger goes back to our Puritan heritage. While the subject of anger is not a primary topic in American Puritan literature, the notion is implied that anger, except righteous indignation against sin, is not to be tolerated.

Indeed, a passive or even cheerful acceptance of life at its hardest is to be sought. "The more it hurts the better it is" is sometimes the standard of godliness. Certainly to be angry at pain would be to destroy the reward of the virtue of enduring it!

John Cotton, a primary spokesman for the American Puritan movement, wrote in 1641: "Fourthly, another act of faith about a man's vocation is this: It encourageth a man in his calling to the most homeliest and difficultest and most dangerous things his calling can lead and expose himself to."[2]

There are many fine values and many areas of sensitivity to the will of God expressed in Puritan literature; yet there is an undercurrent of praising pain and suppressing anger that is deeply imbedded in our American culture to this day. If a medicine is bitter or a job difficult, it must be worthwhile! While we are a violent, angry society partly because we have lost much of what was positive in our Puritan heritage, we individually deny that anger in ourselves. It is easier to say society is angry than to admit I am angry.

Christians many times have strong hang-ups about anger, for they often combine the condemning attitude of the society in which they live with an overspiritualization of their own making.

A rather plainly dressed teenage girl with a look of desperateness written across her face walked into my office and began examining my religious beliefs.

"Do you believe in the Trinity?"

"Is Jesus God?"

"What about the virgin birth? Can you accept that?"

"Are you really a Christian?" "Really saved?" "Are you sure?"

While answering affirmatively, I was growing a little annoyed at this inquisition—and slightly bored. After all, who was she? I had never seen her before. Where in the world did she come from?

Then suddenly her mood changed. More sure of me, she

began to pour out anger regarding her father, a minister.

"I hate him," she ended. "He's never once really talked with me, and he's never tried to get to know or like my friends."

Then, as quickly as the anger had come, remorse and guilt set in. "I shouldn't be angry because I'm a Christian. Do you think I'll go to hell?"

For most Christians anger is disturbing. To those who have deep emotional problems, like this minister's daughter, anger becomes a strong force and a great cause of deep, painful guilt problems. At first glance, anger just doesn't seem Christian; yet the Bible is truly a book of divine balance, and Christianity is not so much a bag of rules as it is an explanation of a healthy, real relationship with Jesus Christ. Consistent with this viewpoint is the view the Bible presents regarding anger.

A key verse regarding anger is: "Be ye angry, and sin not: let not the sun go down upon your wrath: Neither give place to the devil" (Eph. 4:26–27). In the Living Bible these verses read: "If you are angry, don't sin by nursing your grudge. Don't let the sun go down with you still angry—get over it quickly; for when you are angry you give a mighty foothold to the devil."

Clearly anger is not sinful; yet how anger is handled may or may not be sinful. In Ephesians the key seems to be "get over it quickly." Anyone familiar with psychosomatic illness would admit that anger held in and kept is a destructive, negative emotion which can cause physical illness. That quiet man who never retaliates when his wife nags at him may not be so godly as unable to face and handle anger, and he may be a perfect candidate for a heart attack or stroke in a few years. He would be better off to face his anger and "get over it quickly," which can only be done through some kind of outward expression.

The Bible is full of examples of anger—constructive and destructive. Probably God was first in the biblical record to feel anger when he expelled Adam and Eve from the Garden of Eden.

In the Old Testament the life of Moses provides graphic

illustrations of the biblical view of constructive and destructive ways of handling anger. At one point in his leadership of Israel, Moses failed to calm a rebellion in the camp of the Israelites after they had left Egypt to go to the land God had promised. Some of the men accused Moses, saying, "You brought us out of lovely Egypt to kill us here in this terrible wilderness" (Num. 16:13, LB). Keeping in mind that in "lovely Egypt" they had been slaves of the king, beaten and mistreated, it is no wonder Moses responded in anger: "Then Moses was very angry and said to the Lord, "Do not accept their sacrifices!' " (Num. 16:15, LB).

To Moses' surprise, God's anger outdid his: "Get away from these people so that I may instantly destroy them" (Num. 16:21, LB).

At that point Moses pleaded to God: "Must you be angry with all the people when one man sins?" (Num. 16:22, LB). And God relented.

None of this anger was sin; yet both Moses and God were angry *and* free in expressing that anger.

In contrast to Moses' good handling of anger in this situation is the time when Moses out of anger went against God. God said to Moses, " 'Take the elders of Israel with you and lead the people out to Mt. Horeb. I will meet you there at the rock. Strike it with your rod—the same one you struck the Nile with —and water will come pouring out, enough for everyone!' Moses did as he was told, and the water gushed out!" (Exod. 17:5–6, LB).

Later, however, the Israelites were again complaining that there was not enough water to drink. "A great mob formed, and they held a protest meeting. . . . 'You have deliberately brought us into this wilderness to get rid of us, along with our flocks and herds. Why did you ever make us leave Egypt?' " (Num. 20:2–5, LB).

Reacting properly, Moses once again turned to God with his dilemma, and God once again instructed him how to get water.

But this time Moses was clearly *not* to strike the rock but to speak to it.

With seeming calm Moses got the rod and called the people as God had instructed him. Then in a burst of anger, Moses said: " 'Listen you rebels! Must we bring you water from this rock?' Then Moses lifted the rod and struck the rock twice, and water gushed out; and the people and their cattle drank" (Num. 20: 10–11, LB).

However, the result in Moses' life was condemnation from God. In his anger he had ignored God's command and struck the rock—not only once but twice. It was an act which many commentators feel has deep theological significance in biblical typology and thus a serious offense. Consequently, Moses was deprived of the ultimate privilege of leading the Israelites into the promised land although he was allowed to see it at a distance.

The obvious teaching regarding anger in the life of Moses is that anger in itself is not wrong; nor is expressing anger wrong. It is the mode of expression that is important.

On a more contemporary level, Marie, a woman in her late fifties, walked into my office some time ago. Her life had been difficult; she was frustrated, angry, searching for answers. Early in her marriage her husband had left her with a five-year-old daughter. The child visited him weekly until Marie discovered he was doping her child with wine and then molesting her. Marie's other contacts with men had been equally destructive; she had deteriorated from the already insecure person she was as a child to a desperate older woman. She angrily blamed her background and society for all her problems, and for a while it was necessary for her to express that anger freely. At some point it was also important for her to accept responsibility for the present and begin to build her life, using anger positively in the process.

Marie was able to do much in the way of changing her life; yet even in her anger she had not sinned. She felt the anger and expressed it and then moved on in a healthy direction. Real bitterness never developed because she didn't nurture her hostile feelings.

Later, however, her sister, Janice, came to see me. Janice had been brought up in the same poisoned environment as Marie, and Janice was extremely bitter. A much younger woman of thirty-three, Janice took out her wrath in a variety of destructive ways. She beat her two children, she quarreled with her co-workers at a local bank, and she was ready to hate me before she met me.

"Marie thinks you're so great," she started, "but I'm not as easy to fool. You don't care about Marie and you can't help me!" She was *partially* right. While I did care a great deal about Marie, it was hard to get interested in Janice and almost impossible to help her. It is difficult to like someone who is throwing anger at you. Not only had Janice's anger hurt innocent people, which is always wrong, but it was a roadblock between her and others and was thus self-destructive as well.

Apart from the biblical fact of anger is being an appropriate emotion at times, depending on how it is expressed, the Bible also says that God is slow to become angry (see Neh. 9:17). The word *slow* here does not mean inability, but it connotes self-control. As far as we humans are concerned, the way we handle anger is based largely on our self-concept. If I feel sure about myself and comfortable in my own presence, then unfair jabs and the hostility of others will not threaten me as quickly. And once angry, it will certainly be easier for me to recover than if I already have serious self-doubts. Conversely, a good self-image will not easily permit a person to be walked over. One may be *slow* to anger, but at some point if he or she is pushed too far, anger will develop. This is unlike the person with a low self-image who explodes with anger too quickly or holds it in and is perhaps never fully conscious of its presence.

A man who becomes insanely jealous and angry when he sees his wife talking to another man does not have a good self-image.

In contrast, the man who reacts to his wife's unfaithfulness with "I don't blame her; I haven't much to offer" is also deficient in self-esteem. He is afraid to be angry, he doesn't feel he is worth an angry reaction. *Slowness* to anger is, therefore, one sign of a good sense of self-worth, and self-worth fluctuates even within one person.

For several years I counseled groups of tenth-graders. There were about thirty-five in each group, and the demands were great, but I loved doing it and felt effective enough to have a fair amount of confidence. The groups lasted for ten weeks, at the end of which I usually passed out evaluation sheets and had the teenagers discuss what they liked and didn't like about the program. There was enough positive feedback to make me feel confident; so negative comments either indicated areas to work harder on or reflected the isolated disagreement of a single student. My self-confidence in that program helped me use criticism constructively and prevented me from too many angry reactions. My attitude probably showed itself to the students because I can remember several of them kidding me about never getting mad.

In contrast, however, one day a group didn't go well; I was tired and edgy. All I needed was one girl, whom I normally liked, to keep talking while I was trying to get a point across. I stopped suddenly and spent three or four minutes telling her directly how rude she was. Rude she had been, but not *that* rude, and when I cooled down, I apologized, an act which actually strengthened our relationship. Yet if my self-image had not been down that day, I would never have been that quickly angered. I wasn't feeling secure, and so I behaved out of my insecurity.

My reaction was, I am afraid, typical of many authority figures. We tend to be quick to anger, and when we feel angry and can't find an appropriate outlet, it is easy to let anger out at someone who can't easily fight back—an employee, a child, a husband or a wife, a student, or an animal. That is one reason it is important to develop ways of coping with anger at home and on the job. Those are two places where anger can be very destructive if used incorrectly.

Part of what makes a psychologically healthy person slow to anger is sensitivity to the offending party. When a paranoid schizophrenic patient accused me of poisoning his coffee, I did not react with anger because I knew he was living in delusions. Actually it was amazing that he trusted me as much as he did. But if a friend to whom I am close should suddenly accuse me of betrayal, then I would be hurt and probably angry.

Christ himself was slow to anger with the woman caught in adultery because he knew her heart, and he reacted quickly against her accusers because he also knew their inner thoughts. He showed anger at the disciples when they tried to keep the children from him, and yet he was tender when the multitudes pressed against him. In violent anger he chased the money changers out of the temple, but he showed only a weary disappointment when the disciples slept while he prayed in the Garden of Gethsemane.

The most significant example of slowness to anger in the history of mankind was exhibited two thousand years ago by Jesus. Christ, the God-man, crucified by the caprice of a mob and the weakness of those in authority, prayed with agonized genuineness, "Father, forgive these people, . . . for they don't know what they are doing" (Luke 23:34, LB). His profound comprehension of the significance of what he was doing contrasted with the total ignorance of the crowds. His sensitivity to them and their plight helped make him slow to anger indeed.

Anger is not an emotion we can ignore or eliminate. It is, however, a feeling that can be channeled and used for good; it need not be the destructive force we often observe on TV. Above all, it is not a feeling to hide or repress as something sinful for which God is waiting to punish us. I do not believe God is as repressive as some legalistic Christians would have us think.

In *Mere Christianity* C. S. Lewis said:

There is a story about a schoolboy who was asked what he thought God was like. He replied that, as far as he could make out, God was, "The sort of person who is always snooping around to see if anyone is enjoying himself and try to stop it." And I am afraid that is the sort of idea that the word Morality raises in a good many people's minds; something that interferes, something that stops you having a good time.[3]

God is not waiting to stop us from having a good time; nor does he condemn human feelings. He accepts our humanity, including our anger. What he does demand is us, for we, not our anger, are the focus of his attention. When he has us, he can turn all our emotions in the right direction. God has the power to use anger positively, but it is not enough to give him our anger.

Recently I felt a deep need for God's help with a problem in my life, and so I met with some friends with whom I frequently pray. As we talked, I had a growing conviction that what I most deeply wanted was not the answer to my problem but God's complete involvement in my life. I didn't give up asking for God's help, but I refocused on my need to be totally committed to him. Relief in knowing that the total me belonged completely to him was deeply satisfying, and God did answer our prayers regarding the specific problem. What I learned anew and more deeply was how important it is for me to be daily, moment-by-moment, committed to Jesus Christ.

As Lewis said:

> The Christian way is different: harder, and easier. Christ says, "Give Me all. I don't want so much of your time and so much of your money and so much of your work: I want you . . ." Give up yourself, and you will find your real self. Lose your life and you will save it. Submit to death, death of your ambitions and favorite wishes every day and death of your whole body in the end: submit with every fibre of your being, and you will find eternal life. Keep back nothing. Nothing that you have not given away will ever really be yours. Nothing in you that has not died will ever be raised from the dead. Look for yourself, and you will find in the long run only hatred, loneliness, despair, rage, ruin, and decay. But look for

Christ and you will find Him, and with Him everything else thrown in.[4]

NOTES

1. Haim Ginott, "I Am Angry! I Am Appalled! I Am Furious!" *Today's Education—NEW Journal,* November 1972, p. 23.

2. John Cotton, "The Way of Life," *American Heritage,* ed. Leon Howard, Louis B. Wright, and Carl Brode (Boston: D. C. Heath and Co., 1955), 1:25.

3. C. S. Lewis, *Mere Christianity* (New York: Macmillan, 1960), p. 64.

4. Ibid., p. 188.

3

Childhood Anger

Eight-year-old Mary sat close to me in the large overstuffed chair in my office. It was "her hour" as she put it, and she watched the clock begin to erode her sixty minutes. "Maybe the clock doesn't work," she commented hopefully.

Mary had lived for eight years with a father who took excessive amounts of pills and with a mother who regularly shot up with heroin. Now Mary's mother had been hospitalized for an overdose, and her father had mysteriously disappeared.

Out of guilt her parents had brought Mary to see me. In the month we had talked, Mary and I had become close; yet there was usually a sad remoteness about her which one sees more often in older people who have suffered deeply. Today was different. The distance was gone, and all Mary did was cry while I held her very tightly. During most of her eight years crying had been a forbidden privilege, something for which she had been spanked instead of comforted. Responding to my touch and willingness to let her express her feelings, once in a while between sobs she would choke out, "I love you."

A few months earlier I had met another child. Michelle was six and had been raised by parents who considered her a nuisance and had even ignored many of her basic physical needs. When she was a small baby, there were times when she was not fed or changed for twenty-four hours. Yet both parents were bright and well educated. They finally admitted to me that they wished she had never been born for she had interrupted their free life-style.

The first child, Mary, cried to be with her mother and father even though they had physically abused her. In spite of their behavior, in their own sick way they had loved Mary. Michelle, while she had not been physically injured, had effectively gotten the message that she was not loved and therefore that she was not worth loving. Sometimes, being abused and yet noticed is less psychologically destructive than neglect.

Yet both children felt angry, for it is impossible to be either abused or neglected without feeling anger and at times deep rage. Two of the greatest causes of childhood anger are abuse and neglect. Being physically hurt by parents who are supposed to love you is unfair and causes one to feel rejected which in turn creates anger. Furthermore, physical pain itself is anger producing. For example, an adult who stubs a toe or hits a finger with a hammer reacts angrily. People shout at doors they run into, as if the door could hear. Neglect creates anger because indifference says to a child, "You're bad, you're not worth loving, you're not even worth my time!"

While it may be difficult for most of us to relate to gross neglect and abuse, minor incidents and subtle attitudes involving these qualities also contribute to childhood anger. Throwing away your oldest son's torn bluejeans, which have taken him months to break in, may seem like a sensible act, but to him it comes through as not caring enough about his feelings to consult him or listen to him. Neglect of personal feelings creates anger.

A small child wandered away from her mother in the grocery store. In two-year-old fashion she began to finger the brightly wrapped packages of hard candies. "Jodie, don't you dare touch those," her mother shouted in a penetrating voice that caused more notice than the child's actions would have caused. Then came the spanking—public, severe, and unwarranted, an act of parental rage, not discipline. The result was rage in the child who had been abused, not in a legal, technical sense, but in terms of mistreatment and humiliation. Her mother found it difficult to understand why, later in the day, Jodie began to stutter. The mother had forgotten the grocery store incident, but Jodie was still very angry. Her rage manifested itself in stuttering.

Verbal abuse can also cause deep, pervasive anger. A young mother once shouted on the phone to me, "I wish I had never had these kids!" A four-year-old and a six-year-old stood by listening. Another parent said to her teenage daughter, "You'll never make it. You've never made it at anything." Or, more typically, I hear statements like "You're just like your father" (who had just gone on an alcoholic binge) and, in front of the child, "I'm afraid he takes after the bad side of the family!"

Besides abuse and neglect, other factors nurture childhood anger. Unfairness is a paramount cause. The child who brought gifts to everyone else's birthday party felt cheated when her mother told her friends not to bring gifts to her party. The adult explanation of "I don't want your friends to feel obligated" did not satisfy the child. She felt cheated and was depressed and angry during the party.

Adults who lie to their children also contribute to a son's or daughter's anger. One ten-year-old was repeatedly told by his father that his parents would soon live together again. Six months was given as a deadline. Nine months later John confronted his father. "Why did you lie to me?" he asked angrily. "You promised to come back and you lied." In sheer rage, John's father kicked his foot through the child's door. John, helpless in the face of such intense emotion, apologized, an act which only amplified the unfairness of the adult world and intensified his anger.

Adding to the frustration such children experience is a child's helplessness in defending himself or herself. A father who was very angry at his estranged wife took his ten-year-old son out for dinner and a baseball game. Using his son as a sounding board, he inaccurately accused the boy's mother of running around with other men and of being a bad mother and wife. Confused, the boy later said to me: "I feel like my two best friends are fighting, and I'm in between. But it's different from friends my own age because I can't tell my parents to shut up. All I feel is bottled-up and angry."

Symptoms which reflect anger in a child are varied. Some throw a kicking, screaming tantrum that humiliates the parents in front of their friends who already think the parents have been too permissive. Others become depressed, withdraw, and wish to die. Both are angry reactions, but they look quite different to the outside world.

Stuttering is sometimes an unrecognized symptom of anger in children as are certain types of hyperactivity and bullying. Some children steal to get back at an adult world with whom they are angry. Unfortunately, children do not have enough self-awareness or verbal facility to accurately identify their feelings and express them in words. Therefore it is especially difficult for them to appropriately handle anger.

Yet anger can be and often is used positively even by children. A young teenage girl who had an extremely brilliant older sister was constantly denigrated by her family for "not achieving as well in school as Sally did." Karen responded by secretly destroying her sister's belongings, shouting at the whole family, and eventually running away from home. As Karen and I talked, we tried to figure out ways she could not only handle her anger but also stop her sister's harassment. Karen finally realized that if she could turn anger into a positive assertiveness which would stop her sister from walking over her she would be on top of the situation.

A few days after we talked, Sally quipped snidely, "Too bad

your grades are so rotten, Karen. Oh, well, mine make up for both of us!"

Infuriated, but keeping cool, Karen retorted, "Don't worry about it, Sally. I have a lot of things in my life that make me as happy as getting high grades."

Confused because she didn't get the usual sputtering, helpless but angry response, Sally began to learn that teasing Karen wasn't fun anymore. After all, what fun is teasing unless you really get a rise out of the person?

The two girls will probably never be close. They are just too different, but a quiet respect is beginning to develop between them. And Karen is less hostile because she is learning to use her anger well.

At times the key to a child's social success at school depends on how well he or she handles anger. Tommy had always been mischievous and frequently seemed to be in trouble. He appeared to be one of those youngsters who always gets in trouble, always gets caught, and even manages to be blamed unjustly for other children's misbehavior. After a series of such incidents he was brought to me. The school had almost decided to expel him.

"It's not fair," he shouted. "Nobody else ever gets caught." In a way he was right, but he also had to realize several truths: His behavior *was* unacceptable a good part of the time; he had a choice in changing that behavior; and his anger could increase his difficulty in succeeding at school. On the other hand, he could choose to turn his anger toward proving he was a person who could achieve. His reputation and his getting along were in his control.

Tommy's first excuse to me was, "It won't work. Even if I'm good, nobody will believe me."

Bluntly I responded with, "You're right, at first they won't and maybe that's unfair, but you gave them reason to doubt you in the first place. Now give them time to believe you've changed. Be angry enough to prove them wrong!"

Challenged in this way, Tommy worked hard. He was right.

No one believed him at first, but soon one and then another person realized that Tommy was becoming a different person. After several months he not only had more friends his own age but teachers liked him and his grades improved.

Ultimately, however, the parent plays the most integral role in influencing how a child deals with anger and how much actual anger he or she experiences. Childhood anger largely relates to the surrounding adult world.

Essential to helping a child handle his or her anger is the ability on the part of the parent to do the same with his or her feelings of hostility. An angry parent who cannot face, control, and use his or her anger will not be able to help a child in this area. Worse still, the parent may actually contribute to the child's anger.

A thirteen-year-old boy, Joe, is negligent about cleaning his room; yet he has an inventive, creative mind, a spiritual potential far beyond his years, and a personality that immediately draws one to him. Blind to all these qualities, his father, a successful accountant, told me bluntly: "His room is a mess. I can't stand the boy. He will never be the equal of his older brother." Joe *is* the equal of his older brother and will continue to be unless some day he destroys his potential with an anger that is growing to dangerous proportions. His rage is the direct outgrowth of a father who, unsatisfied with his own life and myopic to the varied positive qualities in his son, provokes and eggs him on until Joe lives in a constant state of rage.

Contrary to some popular current thinking, Joe's father does *not* have the right to damage his son in this way. Parents do not possess or own their children. To the contrary, children are entrusted to parents to be raised toward self-sufficiency and dependence on God. They are not the property of the parents, for they are owned only by God, and one must be very careful indeed about handling God's property. Such a concept is scriptural. At age twelve Jesus demonstrated the priority of his allegiance to God. He disappeared from his parents in the temple with the explanation: "I must be about my Father's business."

As an adult, Jesus talked about the worth of a child and the dire danger of hurting children:

> At the same time came the disciples unto Jesus, saying, Who is the greatest in the kingdom of heaven?
>
> And Jesus called a little child unto him, and set him in the midst of them,
>
> And said, Verily I say unto you, Except ye be converted, and become as little children, ye shall not enter into the kingdom of heaven.
>
> Whosoever therefore shall humble himself as this little child, the same is greatest in the kingdom of heaven.
>
> And whoso shall receive one such little child in my name receiveth me.
>
> But whoso shall offend one of these little ones which believe in me, it were better for him that a millstone were hanged about his neck, and that he were drowned in the depth of the sea (Matt. 18:1–6).

The word *offend* in this passage comes from a Greek word meaning "to trip up," "to occasion to fall."

The apostle Paul expressed a similar concept: "Fathers, provoke not your children to anger, lest they be discouraged" (Col. 3:21).

H. C. G. Moule's rendering of this verse is striking:

> Parents do not irritate your children, do not challenge their resistance by unwise and exacting interferences, so different from the steady firmness of thoughtful and responsible affection, that they may not be out of heart, discouraged under the chilling feeling that it is impossible to please, that the word of praise is never heard, that confidence is never reposed in their affection and fidelity.

With more emphasis on the anger-potential in children, Paul wrote to the Ephesians: "And, ye fathers, provoke not your children to wrath" (Eph. 6:4).

In Greek the word *provoke* in the Colossians reference means "to stimulate (especially to anger)." According to Jamieson,

Fausset, and Brown the word *provoke* can be translated "irritate not." In the Ephesians reference a different Greek word is used meaning "to anger alongside, to enrage."

The Scriptures balance the parents' responsibility with the child's obligation to honor his or her parents—but in the Lord. Parents are certainly given no license to own children or to contribute to a damaging anger that can result in the myriad of symptoms previously mentioned.

In contrast to the idea of provoking children to anger, a parent's role should include encouragement. Angry children often have a defective self-image which is further damaged by parental anger or parental passivity. Encouragement, on the other hand, can raise the child's sense of self-worth and alleviate his anger.

John was twelve, just about to enter seventh grade, and very unsure of himself. He was still a little boy whose mother had decorated his room with Teddy bears and electric trains. But he was also becoming a teenager who wanted to throw all that "junk" away and have a room which would establish his identity with his other prejunior-high friends. Reluctantly his parents gave him permission to do his room.

The result was a parent's nightmare but an adolescent boy's dream. Down came the well-framed paintings, up went motorcycle posters and signs with arrows and words like *stop* and *off limits*. Motorcycle helmets decorated the once functional desk. Strange sounds began to emanate from the stereo which had put in many more years playing "Winnie the Pooh." The final addition was a moderately small snake who slithered around in a glass tank and ate live mice.

Then came the grand tour. John's mother took one look and started to cry. "Isn't it awful," she blurted out. Although John was bright enough to know his mother could not be expected to appreciate the new decor, he had hoped she'd at least tolerate it and maybe commend him on the neatly arranged shelves, the vacuumed rug, and the dusted furniture. At least the room was clean!

Anger began to boil inside John. He had put in a lot of hard work, and, after all, they *had* said he could do what he wanted. As his father entered the room, John was ready for anything. For a moment his father just stood there, getting his bearings. Then putting one arm comfortingly around his wife, he turned to John and said, "You've worked hard, and I'm sure it's going to be a great room for you while you're in junior high." John's anger retreated, and a feeling of proud accomplishment came over him. The day would come when he too would think the room a little too much, but that would be much later when he was older. Right now he felt the encouragement of a father who really didn't *like* the room at all but who understood and recognized the work and ingenuity that had been put into it.

John had been encouraged in two ways. First, his parents had trusted him enough to let him develop a room which reflected his identity at that point in his life. Trust like that says, "I believe in you. I accept you as a separate individual with rights and feelings unique to you."

Second, John received affirmation of what he had created from his father—and eventually from his mother when she understood.

Paralleling this illustration, Dr. Tournier comments:

> Sooner or later, the child must either run the risk of neurosis or free himself from his parents and follow his own devices, his own tastes, his own inclinations. Few parents welcome this awakening of individuality in their children. Almost all of them suggest to their children that it is wrong to like what their parents dislike, to desire what they disapprove of or to behave otherwise than they expect. . . .
>
> By their behaviour as much as by their words, austere living parents suggest that anything that gives pleasure is sinful! Many people have told me how this idea from their upbringing has lingered on. It was inculcated like an inexorable adage: "Enjoyment prohibited." They can enjoy nothing without feeling conscience-stricken and this spoils their pleasure.[1]

Angry children often lack trust and affirmation from their homes, and so instead of decreasing, anger snowballs and increases.

At this point some parent may well say, "But I don't like my son's music or my daughter's cut-off jeans and beer T-shirt. I don't like the way they dress or the decor of their rooms since they started to grow up." And with them I would heartily concur; yet there is a way of accepting without liking.

Some teenage friends insisted I listen to their newest rock record. Reluctantly I agreed, only because I knew it was important to them. When they finished, they anxiously asked, "Did you like it?"

"Not really," I admitted, "but listen to mine." I played an Andre Crouch record which a lot of teenagers do like, but not my friends. They didn't like Andre Crouch any more than I liked their hard rock. A little mystified, we agreed it wasn't important. After all, we wouldn't have become friends to start with if there wasn't much in each of us that we all really liked. We were honest and yet accepting in our disagreement. No one felt put down although we may have doubted each other's musical taste!

Agreeing that encouragement is a good antidote for anger and that rejection fosters anger, we are compelled to face the importance of one of the most subtle forms of communication —body language. A brittle tone of voice and stiff body movements can be as rejecting as words; a smile, a touch of the hand, a wink at the right moment during stress can all say much in the way of encouragement and acceptance.

In addition to a general positive attitude toward a child, a parent may do several simple, practical things to help his or her child deal with anger. Just as the parent accepts the fact that to feel anger is both normal and right, this fact must be conveyed directly to the child. One child plied me with questions: "Are you ever angry?"

"Yes."

"Were you angry when you were my age?"

"Sometimes. Everyone feels anger. It's okay."

"Oh! Well . . . did you ever get angry at your parents?"

"Yes, but I can't remember details."

"Oh good! Then it's okay to be really angry at my mother at times?"

"Yes, of course."

Much relieved the child went back to her play as though a great load had been lifted. Children need to be told that we adults feel anger, that they can feel hostile, and that God doesn't condemn those feelings.

What is *done* with angry feelings is another side of the coin, however. Once again much responsibility lies with the parent in helping the child handle the anger he or she now knows is okay to feel. First, the parent will be an example. He or she follow the basic principle that it is okay to be angry as long as you don't hurt anyone with that anger.

A young father came home livid after being demoted at work. He screamed out his rage at his wife while his three-year-old son, not fully comprehending the scene, sat idly by. As the little boy gazed out the window, he saw a scene which amused him and grinned. Suddenly he felt a sharp sting across his face. His father had slapped him for "finding humor in such serious family problems." The child was never sure quite what had happened, but one thing was certain: it would be hard for that father to teach his son we shouldn't hurt people with our anger. The example spoke louder than any words.

Besides being an example, a parent can often actively encourage a child to talk out angry feelings and perhaps get rid of them. A teenage girl cut two hours of school to help a friend. When she got caught, she couldn't begin to defend herself without hurting the friend who already had enough problems. So she kept quiet. The result? A phone call home from the school and a day's suspension.

Laura was boiling with anger. In her mind it all seemed so

unfair. She conjured up in her mind what she could do to get back at the vice-principal, but fortunately her parents finally believed in her enough to ask, "What really happened, Laura?" And Laura trusted them enough to tell them. They respected her decision not to tell on her friend, and so the school never knew the truth and she was suspended. But those people who meant the most to her knew, and that made her feel much less angry. Talking out her anger and finding acceptance drained off a rage that could have been spent lashing out unfairly at someone or even in destructive activity.

Sometimes parents with an angry child don't have the same close parent-child relationship that existed in Laura's family. There are so many possible reasons a child might not be willing to talk to his or her parents that no one needs to feel guilty, but it is important that the child be able to talk to someone. Often a close relative or friend is available. Sometimes professional counseling may be the outlet needed to ventilate the child's anger and help reestablish the relationship in the home.

Above all, parents impart to their children a great gift if they can help them learn to use anger as a positive, motivating force. Children who fail a subject in school and feel anger because the grade seems unjust have two choices: give up and wallow in self-pity or take that anger and prove how much better they can do next time. A child unjustly criticized by a neighbor for ruining a flower garden that he or she wasn't even near can hate the neighbor forever or can start to prove that he or she is a much better person than the neighbor thinks.

A parent's attitude greatly influences the child's decision. Blaming the school in a way that implies the child has no chance to succeed, joining in on hating the neighbor—both attitudes reinforce the child's feeling that he or she is helplessness to change things. Helplessness, in turn, creates anger. A parent who says, "I understand your anger, but there are some things you can do," positively helps his or her child not only to handle anger but to *use* it for good.

In some ways anger is a confusing emotion for adult and child. It can be destructive, or it can be the motivation upon which to build great successes. It can create bitter, disagreeable, dangerous people, or it can toughen and motivate people to do things they never dreamed of before. Childhood anger is important because how a child handles anger will determine how that child grown up will use feelings of hostility.

Catherine Marshall in her book *Beyond Our Selves* tells the gripping story of a young man, Harvey, who tried in various heroic ways to help his friend only to be knifed severely in the chest and abdomen. Rushed to the hospital, Harvey was in surgery for almost eight hours and then for days lived precariously close to death. Through his belief in Christ he was able in his semiconscious state to say, "Jack, I forgive you."

A few weeks later his doctor had a significant conversation with Harvey.

"You're going to get well," she told him one morning.

The patient smiled at her. "I've known that for several days. It's mostly thanks to you, too."

"No-o. There's another reason. Your condition has been so precarious that anything could have tipped the scales."

"What do you mean?"

"I've watched you closely. You've been at peace with yourself, especially the last ten days. If you had held on to any hate at all, that negative emotion would have sapped so much of your energy that you probably would not have pulled through."

Throughout the rest of the day, Harvey pondered the doctor's words. In this case, hateful unforgiving thoughts would literally have destroyed him.[2]

Such is the potential for destruction in a misuse of anger —and the opportunity for even miracles when anger is handled well. Once again, such is the wisdom of the biblical injunction to be angry but sin not.

NOTES

1. Paul Tournier, *Guilt and Grace* (New York: Harper & Row, 1962), p. 12.

2. Catherine Marshall, *Beyond Our Selves* (New York: McGraw-Hill, 1961), p. 130.

4

Using Anger in Relationships

When Joanne first walked into my office, I had difficulty believing she was upset. A well-groomed look, expensive clothes, a smiling face, and a cheerful hello made her appear one of the world's fortunate. Then she started to talk.

Still smiling, she told me about her two children: One severely mentally retarded child lived in an institution, and a teenage daughter was having some heavy emotional problems.

Her husband, Jerry, was a bright, hard-working accountant who never knew when to quit and come home. "Yet I understand," Joanne reassured me. "He works hard, and sometimes there's not much to come home to"—still the smile on her face! I wondered if she would ever *look* like what she felt. She was telling me a lifelong tragedy with a smile.

Finally I asked, "Do you and Jerry ever argue or fight?"

With a sudden, fleeting look of horror, she quickly answered, "No, what would we argue about?"

"What would we argue about?" Joanne had ulcers. Her physician attributed her condition to repressed negative feelings. Neither parent could communicate with their daughter. Jerry had been impotent for about three years, but he and Joanne never discussed their sex problems. Buried in his work, Jerry felt his office had become a kind of haven-escape, and Joanne felt alone and neglected at home. Each was hurting and each was angry; yet with each other they were polite and basically non-communicative.

Oh, once in a while the anger spurted. Like when Jerry sarcastically remarked about their daughter, "*You* should be able to talk to her; you're her mother." Or worse still, when Joanne retaliated with, "The least you could do is function like a man." Yet it was useless, destructive anger that produced nothing but guilt and more anger.

As I got to know both Jerry and Joanne, I found them nice people who had little access to their own feelings and much less to the emotions of each other. At first they both flatly denied even *feeling* angry, and Joanne continued to look pleasant.

Slowly they became more real. Jerry admitted he hated holing up in his office eighteen hours a day and that he felt put down by Joanne for his sexual impotence. Joanne described her loneliness and her feeling of guilt that perhaps she wasn't attractive enough to turn Jerry on sexually—or worse still, her fear that he had found another woman.

As they began to face themselves and each other, there was anger, not just flashes of hostility but real feelings of rage. However, they didn't attack; out of pain they communicated. Joanne confronted Jerry with her loneliness, her hurt over the children, and her consequent need for him. Because she was so angry, Jerry believed her, and for the first time in their marriage he really felt needed at home. Jerry told Joanne the anger he felt when she insisted on sexual intercourse and then put him down for not coming through. Realizing for the first time *his* hurt rather than her own, Joanne became supportive instead of castrating which put the couple well on their way to solving their sexual problems.

What emerged in our discussions was the reality of their once-repressed anger. When Jerry and Joanne began to use that anger for honest confrontation, it became the constructive motivation for growth in a relationship between two people who really cared about each other.

In a relationship anger can be a dynamic, destructive force, or those involved can mold the anger into a creative force that promotes personal and relational growth.

I was awakened one morning around 2:30 A.M. by the sharp ringing of the phone. After fumbling around in the dark, I finally grabbed the receiver and heard the hysterical voice of a friend who had lost her husband a few weeks earlier. I thought she had been through the worst of the experience, but apparently I was wrong.

After she had talked through her feelings for quite a while, she pleaded, "Please talk to me about something happy. Tell me what you did today, something you enjoyed."

After groping around for what to say, I told her how excited I was about an idea for a magazine article I was in the middle of writing.

There was dead silence. Then, "How can you dare to be so happy when I'm so miserable!" Stunned by her irrational answer, I didn't say anything for a minute. Then I suggested that if she wasn't strung out any more we both get to sleep.

I lay awake for a while wondering, angry. The next day when I knew she could handle it better I confronted her with what she had said and with my anger over what I considered her selfishness and self-indulgence. Two positive things arose from that confrontation. I got rid of my anger which, if it had developed, could have ruined our friendship. My friend learned that even when she hurt badly she could not with impunity lash out and hurt innocent people—even when they cared and were prone to overlook her tendency to do this. The original incident was unfortunate, but the reactions to it strengthened the relationship.

In any close relationship there will be anger. You can't be close without abrasiveness. You can hide it, you can be unaware of it, but from time to time it will pop up. Through examining anger in relationships, how it arises and is expressed, it is possible to develop ways in which the very anger which destroys many relationships can actually become creative.

Focusing anger on the real issue, rather than displacing it on someone or something else, is an important step. A patient with whom I had always maintained a good relationship had been going through a period of self-pity over her position in life. Her husband had died; her only daughter had married and moved away; and most recently, a distant uncle had died and left his entire, rather large fortune to her sister with nothing for her. As a Christian she had felt wrong in engaging in sex with anyone she had dated since her husband's death; yet she felt cheated sexually.

Late one afternoon she sat talking to me about her neighbors' problems with their children. It didn't seem relevant to her life, but I couldn't keep her on any other topic. She seemed to be avoiding a discussion which could relate to her directly. Then suddenly she looked at me with rage.

"You were ten minutes late today," she started in another attempt at diverting the conversation. "I suppose you're losing interest." Upon arriving I had explained that my lateness was due to car trouble, and she had seemed unconcerned. Now it became an issue because she needed a focus for the anger beginning to surface.

"I can't stand people who are late," she continued. "It's a sign of disorganization. You do that again and I'll just quit!"

Resisting the strong urge to tell her to do so, I tried to steer the conversation toward the object of her real anger. Finally, after a near temper tantrum and much displacement of anger, she admitted how much she felt passed by in life and how unloved and unlovable she felt she had become. Her rage now became accurately identified, even to her.

When she faced the real source of her anger, which had nothing to do with me, we could begin to make progress. It was necessary to focus the anger before it could be alleviated and before I or any other human being could help her. As long as *I* was receiving the brunt of her anger, I was becoming too angry to relate to her in a genuine, caring way.

The same is true in a marriage, a family, or a friendship. Displacing anger, putting anger on someone who does not deserve it, makes it impossible to work with the problem causing the anger since it hasn't been identified or faced and because it makes other people angry instead of helpful. The housewife who takes out her rage at her children by yelling at her husband not only does not solve the problem with the children but alienates her husband as well. The man who comes home angry from work and criticizes his wife on some insignificant issue keeps his work problem unsolved and creates a hostile distance between himself and his wife.

In contrast is the husband who comes home at night after a rough day and recognizes his anger. If the children are particularly high strung, he stays away from them until he can handle them without taking out his frustrations on them. And when the house is quiet, he sits down over a cup of coffee and talks out the problems of the day with his wife.

One couple I know never go to bed before they have discussed each of their experiences during that day, good and bad, and then prayed together in detail over what has transpired.

One of the most frequent causes of anger in a relationship revolves around dependency. A friend of mine, Suzanne, asked for help when she found herself drifting into a chronic state of depression. Each morning she found it increasingly unbearable to get out of bed and function. Work bored her; daily tasks became acts involving monumental decisions; her family angered her because their happiness was a constant reminder of how miserable she really was.

Our morning phone conversations and frequent lunches seemed to help at first. She was involved, hard-working, well motivated. She also developed some outside interests with her children. Then, suddenly, precipitously, Suzanne quit calling and seemed to avoid me. Some time later, when one of her children had emergency surgery after an automobile accident, Suzanne called because she needed to talk. In a moment of rare honesty she admitted: "I quit being your friend because I was afraid—afraid of closeness, exposure, and, above all, afraid of being too dependent. It made me angry to need anyone but myself." Still, today, she has no close friends.

The feelings Suzanne experienced were out of proportion to those we feel when we are adequately functioning. We all hesitate to feel vulnerable to another. Still there *is* a vulnerability involved in any good relationship, and most of us accept it. Closeness implies vulnerability, and without it a relationship is distant and meaningless.

Suzanne's overwhelming feelings of dependency made her feel a deep sense of anger. Dependency or even the threat of dependency can cause great anger within a person or within a relationship.

The truth of this is certainly illustrated in the contempt we are shown from countries who receive our foreign aid. Even countries don't like to be dependent, thus the riots and demonstrations against America which often occur. In showing the connection between dependency and anger in the extreme, Dr. Rollo May constructs a striking fictional example. He begins with a question: "What would happen to a person if his freedom were entirely and literally taken away?" Then the story:

> One evening a king of a far land was standing at his window, vaguely listening to some music drifting down the corridor from the reception room in the other wing of the palace. The king was wearied from the diplomatic reception he had just attended, and he looked out of the window pondering about the ways of the world in general and nothing in particular. His eye fell upon a man in the square below—apparently an average man, walking to the corner to take the tram home, who had taken that same route five nights a week for

many years. The king followed this man in his imagination —pictured him arriving home, perfunctorily kissing his wife, eating his late meal, inquiring whether everything was right with the children, reading the paper, going to bed, perhaps engaging in the love act with his wife or perhaps not, sleeping, and getting up and going off to work again the next day.

And a sudden curiosity seized the king which for a moment banished his fatigue, "I wonder what would happen if a man were kept in a cage, like the animals at the zoo?"

So the next day the king called in a psychologist, told him of his idea, and invited him to observe the experiment. Thus the king caused a cage to be brought from the zoo, and the average man was brought and placed therein.

At first the man was simply bewildered, and he kept saying to the psychologist who stood outside the cage, "I have to catch the tram, I have to get to work, look what time it is, I'll be late for work!" But later on in the afternoon the man began soberly to realize what was up, and then he protested vehemently, "The king can't do this to me! It is unjust, and against the laws!" His voice was strong, and his eyes full of anger.

During the rest of the week the man continued his vehement protests. When the king would walk by the cage, as he did every day, the man made his protests directly to the monarch. But the king would answer, "Look here, you get plenty of food, you have a good bed, and you don't have to work. We take good care of you—so why are you objecting?" Then after some days the man's protests lessened and then ceased. He was silent in his cage, refusing generally to talk, but the psychologist could see hatred glowing like a deep fire in his eyes.

But after several weeks the psychologist noticed that more and more it seemed as if the man were pausing a moment after the king's daily reminder to him that he was being taken good care of—for a second the hatred was postponed from returning to his eyes—as though he were asking himself if what the king said were possibly true.

And after a few weeks more, the man began to discuss with the psychologist how it was a useful thing if a man were given food and shelter, and that a man had to live by his fate in any case and the part of wisdom was to accept his fate. So when a group of professors and graduate students came in one day to observe the man in the cage, he was friendly toward them and explained to them that he had chosen this way of life, that there are great values in security and being taken care of, that they would of course see how sensible his course was, and so on. How strange! thought the psychologist, and how pathetic —why is it he struggles so hard to get them to approve of his way of life?

In the succeeding days when the king would walk through the courtyard, the man would fawn upon him from behind the bars in his cage and thank him for the food and shelter. But when the king was not in the yard and the man was not aware that the psychologist was present, his expression was quite different—sullen and morose. When his food was handed to him through the bars by the keeper, the man would often drop the dishes or dump over the water and then be embarrassed because of his stupidity and clumsiness. His conversation became increasingly one-tracked: and instead of the involved philosophical theories about the value of being taken care of, he had gotten down to simple sentences like "It is fate," which he would say over and over again, or just mumble to himself, "It is."

It was hard to say just when the last phase set in. But the psychologist became aware that the man's face seemed to have no particular expression; his smile was no longer fawning, but simply empty and meaningless, like the grimace a baby makes when there is gas on its stomach. The man ate his food, and exchanged a few sentences with the psychologist from time to time; his eyes were distant and vague, and though he looked at the psychologist, it seemed that he never really *saw* him.

And now the man, in his desultory conversations, never used the word "I" any more. He had accepted the cage. He had no anger, no hate, no rationalizations. But he was now insane.

That night the psychologist sat in his parlor trying to write a concluding report. But it was very difficult for him to summon up words, for he felt within himself a great emptiness. He kept trying to reassure himself with the words, "They say that nothing is ever lost, that matter is merely changed to energy and back again." But he couldn't help feeling something *had* been lost, something had been taken out of the universe in this experiment, and there was left only a void.[1]

Good relationships, whether they be within a family structure or between friends, have fluctuating levels of dependency which are healthy. Dependency is one facet of a relationship which, when it goes above a certain level, makes us overly vulnerable while at the same time a reasonable amount of dependency contributes positively. Following a week of hospital testing, I returned home sick and exhausted. After several days I remained tired and somewhat discouraged.

Intuitive friends insisted that I come to their home and rest until the end of the week. For three or four days I slept and ate, doing little else, which is extremely unusual for me since even when I am tired I rarely sleep during the day. I was given steak for breakfast, offered stimulating conversation during my few waking hours, and in general made to feel loved, worthwhile, and wanted. Yet I was dependent on them, at least to a degree, and I contributed little to the friendship. This was an example of positive, good dependency because it was not overly heavy or permanent.

When dependency becomes extreme or extended, however, it engenders the anger and rage Rollo May caricatures in his man-in-the-cage example. The person at that point says, in the words of May, "You have conquered me, but I reserve the right to hate you."[2] A wife who had to account to her husband for every move she made to the point where her phone calls were monitored and her friends scrutinized and restricted came to me in a state of rage. Her big house, fine clothes, and generally easy life meant nothing. All she wanted was to run. Later when John, her husband, talked to me, he said: "I don't understand Sadie. She has everything. I've provided everything this world has to offer." What he had difficulty seeing was that she lacked one essential: freedom. He had bought her and chained her with his money and desires, and the result was hate.

Friends also can imprison each other in a web of dependency needs and generate deep anger. In this situation if either person is at all strong, he or she will probably abandon the friendship.

Jealousy can be a factor. The man who resented best friend's playing golf with someone else put a stranglehold on him to the point where the friendship ended, leaving the first man more devoid of companionship than ever.

Since being dependent can create angry feelings, sensitivity to when dependency needs are becoming too great in a relationship can be a help. People who can do things for themselves are happier and feel more worthwhile. We all need help, and receiving that help makes us feel wanted. But there is a fine line between meeting our needs which makes us feel good about ourselves and depending on others which begins to erode our self-image.

A teenage girl who had never received much love from her family went to live in a foster home. The new family bought her a minimal amount of clothes, gave her her own room, and verbally welcomed her into their home. They were consistently warm, loving, and supportive. When she got a part-time job at school, they let her buy school supplies out of that money, and from the start she did housework equivalent to other members of the family. The first Saturday they all had free they allowed her to take them out for breakfast. She described her relationship with them to me: "I feel grateful for what they're doing, and it makes me feel they care about me. But I don't feel like I'm begging because I carry a lot of my own weight in trying to help whenever I can. I feel I can lean on them, but I also feel I'm doing a good job of coping for myself." It was a good description of a balanced relationship which is far removed from degrading do-gooder programs which give to people and then expect worshipful gratitude in return which only injures the dignity and pride of the individual who has been helped.

Then too a really healthy person does not want to be *depended upon* to the point that his life-style is curtailed or he feels used and walked over. Such a relationship creates anger on both sides, and you can't really help someone when you're angry.

Dependency needs are important in determining the health

and constructiveness of a relationship. In excess, dependency produces an anger which if allowed to grow can destroy an otherwise good relationship but which can also be used for good. Without anger there would be no fighting against dependency, no growth into freedom.

A small child became sick with polio. Once the life-threatening aspects of the disease had diminished, she continued to live in the hospital. For years she received treatment and was the center of consultation and experimentation.

"You can't walk," the doctors finally told her. "Actually, you're going to have a hard time even learning to move your legs again."

Day after day they examined her and talked about her around her bed, oblivious to the fact that Missy was aware of what they were saying and growing angry. She was carried from bed to wheel chair and back to bed. Her anger grew, but it had no outlet. She despised the bed, the braces, the wheel chair, and, above all, the doctors who had become symbols of her dependency.

One day an aunt whom she loved dearly came to visit. "You walk," she said determinedly to Missy.

Suddenly the rage that had built had a focus. Missy would walk! She started by moving one toe, then two, then a foot. Finally, after much struggle and with a continuing, low-keyed anger that pushed her on, she walked. And she has walked ever since—now without braces or crutches. Without anger, however, there would have been no battle against dependency.

In a relationship which includes excessive dependency, there are two alternatives: stay in the relationship without changing and suffer the angry feelings along with fear that the dependency will kill the relationship, or try to develop a degree of self-sufficiency. One way to grow in self-confidence is to channel anger into the motivation to become independent. The little girl who learned to move her toe during her struggle with polio did that. So did the housewife who stopped calling her husband at work every time she had to make a minor decision about her children. The result? Both felt better about themselves. Their self-images went up; they became less dependent; and those they loved respected them more.

Of course, at times there may be adverse reactions to such positive changes. Unquestionably, in the same way that over-dependency can become detrimental in a relationship, so, unfortunately, a growth into better mental health can harm a relationship which is not healthy to start with.

Sometimes, for example, a very dependent wife meets a need in a husband who needs to be needed. He may complain about her constant demands, and she may defy his authoritativeness; but take one away from the other, and they will both be more unhappy. If one of the two becomes truly strong without growth in the other, the relationship will crumble. As the stronger person finds real freedom, the weaker person will have a rough time.

A middle-aged woman came to me for counseling because her marriage was unsatisfying. Her husband ignored the three children and almost never took her to dinner or paid her a compliment. She loved him and wanted the marriage, but she also needed to feel better about herself and her own life.

In subsequent counseling sessions Cheryl learned about liking herself. She developed some genuinely good friendships. She learned to talk to her children and do things with them. Yet her progress concerned me in a way because the happier she became the less she depended on her husband. I could see the marriage crumbling as the wife grew stronger. Her husband, who refused counseling, didn't notice the changes in Cheryl until two weeks before she left him.

Because of the possibility of one person's outgrowing another in a marital relationship, both persons should go into counseling at the same time.

Related to the need for independence in a relationship is the need for space. Everyone needs privacy, time to be alone, opportunity to be themselves; when this is not granted, anger results.

A complaint I frequently hear from businessmen concerns their need for quiet time after a day of pressure. Unfortunately many find this so hard to achieve at home that they seek it in bars. It is difficult after a day of constant pressure to come home and be greeted with "Wait 'til you hear what Johnnie did today" or "What shall we do about our car payment this month?" Even Christ, after dealing with the demands of the multitudes, needed space in which to recover his strength, and so he left the people and all their needs and went to the other side of the lake.

A wife who realizes her husband's need for space will find her relationship with him more fulfilling because he will respect and love her more for that kind of understanding. Conversely, a housewife too needs time for herself. She needs to be able to take a bubble bath and do her nails without the interruptions of a small child. A person on the job twenty-four hours a day, she needs time off. A husband who wants a happy, nonhostile wife will see that she gets space.

What is true in a marriage is also true in any relationship. People need time to breathe, time to be alone. One day last summer I was feeling the pressure of the needs of people around me to the point where I had an angry desire to be left alone. To have allowed those feelings to continue would have led to some poor hours of counseling patients. Instead I allowed my anger to motivate me into taking a much needed day off.

With a friend who also just wanted to be left alone, I packed a lunch, grabbed a favorite book (which is a pickup for me when I'm down), and took off for the ocean.

It was a bright, clear day. There were lots of people, but that didn't matter. I wasn't responsible for them, and so they faded into the background of sand and sky and ocean. I walked on the beach, threw rocks into the water, watched the ripples fade into infinity, and realized that God who created and controlled all this still had his hands firmly on my life.

By sundown my friend and I were hungry and talkative; we

had both had enough solitude. We had each had our own space to breathe in and to shed the residue of life which had temporarily overwhelmed us. Once again we cared about others, about our work, our families, and our friends. Tomorrow would be productive, but today had been ours.

Once in a while we all need such days if we are to avoid becoming angry people, not just people who inevitably feel anger from time to time.

We all too need psychological space, the right to be ourselves and to be accepted. We often choose relationships with people who are like us, but no two people are the same, nor should they be. A friend told me I would be sinning if I went to a church which, although biblically oriented, did not in one aspect agree with her beliefs. She began the destruction of our ten-year friendship. Unless I was like her, she could not be my friend; and unless I could be me, I would not be her friend.

The tendency to mold people probably occurs most often in authority-type relationships such as parent-child, employer-employee, pastor-laity, and even some marriages. If people lose their identity through a relationship, they will be angry. A sign of mental health is to fight such tyranny and to become one's own person or, better still, God's person.

Oversensitivity is one other important facet in an anger-producing relationship. Here too understanding can help. The husband who realizes that a woman becomes supersensitive around her menstrual periods will be less disturbed by her reactions. The wife who understands her husband's business pressures will not be as upset by his moods. Even children have bad days at school, and friends are better for each other one day than another. Yet some people are overly sensitive, and too much touchiness can create anger in a relationship.

A young boy asked to buy a long-desired tool from a neighbor who had one and never used it. Turning to the older man, the boy asked, "How much do I owe you, sir?"

With a grin the man said gruffly, "Beat it."

Insulted, the boy left. When he told his parents the story, they started to laugh. "Why on earth were you upset?" his father asked.

"Because he said 'Beat it,' " replied the boy.

When it was finally explained to him that the man had paid him a high compliment by giving him the tool, the boy felt grateful—and foolish. Such extreme sensitivity can and does harm relationships.

People who constantly ask "Are you angry at me?" "Have you changed in your feelings about me?" "Am I really okay?" irritate others. And there are more subtle ways of expressing excessive need for affirmation. For example saying, "Oh, this is just an old dress," after a compliment implies the need for reinforcement that the dress truly does not look old.

Other factors relate to anger in a relationship. Some are small, but collectively they become large. The house guest who uses your last ounce of shampoo or hair spray without telling you can be infuriating if you end up having to go out and buy some at a highly inconvenient time of night or right before a party. A friend who only calls when he or she has a problem can get by with this some of the time but not always. Neglecting special occasions like birthdays, leaving one's children too often at a friend's, and not keeping your dog in your own yard are not major issues, but spread over a period of time they can become irritating. And irritation is certainly a form of anger.

On the other hand, much anger can be prevented and alleviated by simple considerations. The mother who rented her grown son's room but told him first and assured him he would always have a place to stay when he came home prevented feelings of rejection and anger. The husband who came home after a bad day saying, "I am so frustrated I have nothing left to give," relieved his wife of feeling that she was the cause of his anger.

Probably nothing destroys relationships faster and more effectively than anger; yet perceived quickly and used wisely, it can strengthen a relationship by forcing honesty and change. If an alcoholic can muster enough self-worth to rechannel anger constructively, it can motivate him or her to transfer dependence on a bottle to a person or a group and ultimately to himself or herself and God. Anger can make people want a good marriage instead of a bad one, a healthy friendship instead of no friendship. In this way anger reflects self-worth: "I'm worth more than this situation I have allowed myself to fall into. I can do better than I have in the past."

NOTES

1. Rollo May, *Man's Search for Himself* (New York: W. W. Norton, 1953), pp. 145–48.
2. Ibid., p. 149.

5

A Bad Day at Work

Ruth had always wanted to use the secretarial skills she had carefully cultivated in high school and junior college; yet relinquishing that option for a fulfilling marriage and ultimately several children had never bothered her. After all, no one in this life can do all the things she wishes, and so she was lucky to be happy, she reasoned.

Then came the first shattering blow. Peter, her husband, left her for another woman. An affair had been going on that Ruth had naïvely not suspected although there had been all the danger signals. Peter kept unaccountably late hours and had quite suddenly become sexually disinterested in his wife. Ruth had believed his stories about business pressures, extra required trips, and his utter fatigue. Her children, PTA, the macramé class she taught, and her church activities had kept her so busy that being a wife had unconsciously become secondary.

Hardly recovered from the emotional blow, Ruth found herself thrust into the working world. It was a life she had once coveted, but now it seemed bewildering. Everyone seemed so sure of themselves and had their own place carved out. To Ruth it was all new, but because she was capable, she rose quickly and became secretary to the vice-principal of an elementary school.

After two years, just about the time the pieces of her life were coming together, Ruth received another shattering blow. Both the principal and the vice-principal of the school spontaneously resigned. Since Ruth had never had difficulty relating to people or performing her job activities, her bosses' resignations did not trouble her excessively. She was not worried, that is, until she began to hear rumors that the new administrators preferred new clerical help who would be loyal to them exclusively. According to district policy no one's job could be terminated upon such caprice, but the pressure began to mount. Unreasonable work demands, unfair criticisms, and a lack of positive attitudes made Ruth *want* to quit, which was, of course, the intention.

Ruth's anger mounted. The subtlety and the unfairness made her furious. Yet, much like a small child, she felt helpless to lash back at her superiors who could in turn hurt her professionally. She needed a job, which meant either retaining this one or getting a new one based on a good recommendation from these two men. Rather than blowing up and releasing her anger at them, she quietly stayed out of their way and did her job. Her anger turned into a firm determination to succeed in spite of them; indeed, it became a motivating force. The more she was mistreated, the more she determined she would win, not they.

At the same time Ruth wisely kept her eyes open for other job opportunities, for living forever with excessive amounts of negative emotions is not good for anyone. Eventually that job opportunity came, and Ruth went to her new position with a clean slate from the past.

In contrast, a young man, Marc, saw me briefly because of problems he was having in his job as a restaurant cook. Marc stuttered, and some of the busboys and waitresses constantly teased him. The ridicule was not meant seriously, but understandably it hurt, and unfortunately most people who tease pick on those who react. When Marc would angrily shout out a volley of words in which he stuttered even more than usual or when he would occasionally throw a dish, his tormentors were motivated to continue their harrassment. Because of his uncontrolled anger, Marc lost his job.

Anger led Ruth to a job promotion. With Marc, anger led to the loss of a job. For most of us, anger at work does not usually end in changing jobs. More often we stay where we are and handle or mishandle our anger, for and against our own benefit.

In the first place, most people spend roughly one-third of their lives working, eight hours out of every twenty-four. Unfortunately, as one physician said to me, "So many people I see dislike their jobs and have job-related psychosomatic illnesses."

In general, the anger-producing elements in a job do not outweigh the positive aspects, so most people remain where they are. They enjoy the work; they need the money; or they prefer to avoid unnecessary change. However, most people could cope better than they do with those things in their work environment which irritate them. One way to cope, and thereby avoid internalizing hostility, is don't feed anger with anger, and don't foster situations which produce anger in other people.

I was a young teacher at the time short skirts, colored hosiery, and high boots first became fashionable. One particular employee in the school where I worked had some authority over the types of classes I taught and who was in them. His extreme conservatism and his catering to the "smart kid" or the student with a "good family background" bothered me. In my irritation I made a point of walking into his office on the days I wore pink hose or high boots or short skirts. And he always expressed a proper amount of horror, enough to goad me into shocking him again. My handling of anger in this case was pretty immature, as was his predictable reaction. And in the end it only fed my anger since he had ways of making my schedule difficult which in turn made me just that much more angry.

At another school where I was deeply involved in counseling students who were into drugs, I acted more wisely. These teenagers' needs were often best met by interaction with former addicts and outside drug rehabilitation groups. Therefore at times I invited outside resource people to come on campus and talk with students in groups and individually. Many students' lives were saved, literally, by this program. As one boy said of a former addict, "That man really heard me. He knows where I'm at and makes me feel I can make it after all." Often these resource people came on campus dressed like the strung-out doper, and usually they smoked. This made certain people in the school community very uptight; fortunately those highest in command knew what I was doing and approved. I warded off much irritation by leveling with the outside people; I asked them to dress in a way which made them blend rather than stand out. Most understood and were willing to tone down their vocabulary and smoke off campus. By avoiding unnecessary conflicts, I was able to retain a program that helped many students. I kept any irritation directed at me to a minimum and thus minimized my own anger level. I didn't give up anything important. I just kept petty impulses and reactions out of the picture.

Another way to endure and rise above anger-producing situations in a job is to focus on positive elements both in the job and out of it. A similar approach is advocated by Alvin Toffler in *Future Shock* where he discusses how to compensate for overwhelming change in one's life:

The problem is not, therefore, to suppress change, which cannot be done, but to manage it. If we opt for rapid change in certain sectors of life, we can consciously attempt to build stability zones elsewhere. A divorce, perhaps, should not be too closely followed by a job transfer. Since the birth of a child alters all the human ties within a family, it ought not, perhaps, be followed too closely by a relocation which causes tremendous turnover in human ties outside the family. The recent widow should not, perhaps, rush to sell her house."[1]

The problem is not to suppress or eliminate anger but to manage it. After a bad day at work, compensate by spending an evening with a close friend. I'm fortunate to have two jobs. If I have a hard day with patients, it is restoring to my ego to go home and write. Or, if writing is coming hard, I often enjoy losing myself in the problems of my patients. My dog, music, shopping, a walk on the beach, conversing and praying with a friend I value, reading Robert Browning or C. S. Lewis or Amy Carmichael—for me these are what Toffler calls stability zones. They don't change or hurt me. They remain and they are familiar. They sooth the abrasive pricks of anger into a more even level of determination where I can use my anger constructively rather than allow it to hurt me. They take the edge off anger and restore any loss of self-esteem which may have occurred during the day.

Even within a job, one may discover stability zones. In the second school situation my stability zone was an unusually good principal whose opinion I valued more than the subordinate under her who didn't understand. Often I focused on what was happening with the students themselves. Those who went off drugs or pulled through a difficult experience without being destroyed were positive focal points. Something worthwhile *was* happening. And because achieving that something worthwhile required a different approach, naturally there would be criticism as well as commendation. Keeping my anger minimal allowed me to work still harder at helping teenagers.

Guilt and anger are closely related within a job. I know one history teacher who compulsively administers long essay-type exams, spends disproportionate hours grading them, and stays long hours after school—all because he feels guilty about whether or not he's a good teacher. Then he wonders why he goes home in such a bad mood every night.

Dr. Paul Tournier gives an excellent, deeply relevant illustration of this in *Guilt and Grace:*

> . . . a doctor undertakes with fine zeal the treatment of a difficult case. He extends his researches, examines the literature, has discussions with colleagues and he evinces the most lively solicitude for his patient. But when the patient returns,

despite all, with the same symptoms and the same complaints, the reactions of the doctor undergo a sudden change.

He shows bad temper which upsets the patient. The latter was expecting a still more kindly sympathy, and he is spoken to quite roughly; the doctor even comes to a point of scolding him, of suspecting him of exaggerating his sufferings or of inducing them by disobedience to his instructions. This very often happens with nervous or allergic cases, whose sufferings are difficult to define and even more difficult to overcome, and who react in unexpected ways to drugs.

Neither the doctor nor the patient quite realizes that the storm, so regrettable for the treatment, is due to an unconscious sense of guilt weighing on the doctor's mind. . . .

Who will ever know whether another doctor would have succeeded where I failed? Should I have sent the patient to him instead of proudly taking on the case myself? . . .

. . . The Bible is a school of courage: courage to recognize our wrongdoings; courage also, at times, to stand by our convictions unflinchingly, despite the inevitable sense of guilt which any conflict arouses.

For the Bible also lays upon us the duty of defending ourselves, of not allowing ourselves to be crushed by the judgment of others, by the constant pretention of others to take our place as judges of our conduct and to exercise a moral oversight of our life. In our turn we are called to observe the same reserve towards other people, to resist setting ourselves up as judges of other people's conduct.[2]

There are two appropriate ways to handle guilt and thus deal with the resultant anger. The teacher who was overscrupulous about his work and the doctor who expected perfection and total cures with his patients both needed to face their nonguiltiness. If I do a job well and it doesn't turn out right, I have not failed. As James Lowell wrote, "Not failure but low aim is crime." Or as Browning believed, God values all we aspired to be and could not. We must accept our humanity, for humanity is different from sin. To sin is to go against God. To be human is to fail outwardly even though we give our highest effort. Such failure is not sin nor does it deserve guilt. My friend who tried to walk in spite of a crippling disease and braces and failed was yet never more successful than when she tried at her optimum level. Perhaps much that we feel guilty over we should actually be proud of, as the physician, for example, who takes difficult cases even though he knows he may fail. I know psychotherapists who turn down suicidal cases because they are afraid to fail. Should then another therapist who takes a deeply suicidal patient and loses him after his best efforts feel guilty? Certainly not. He should feel sad, a sense of loss, but not guilt—and hence not a guilt-produced anger.

Of course, at times we commit wrong deeds, feel guilty, and then become angry. Such guilt can only be removed by making right what has been wrong. This side of guilt is more obvious, more discussed, particularly among Christians. It is the unnecessary, unrealistic guilt which often goes unrealized and untreated. Guilt of inadequacy, presumed failure, guilt over past failures, false comparisons with others which place one in an uncomplimentary light all create tension and anger in a job.

Closely related to guilt is the inadequacy some people feel in a job, an inadequacy which is realistic and can be changed. A fellow therapist who discussed with me his frustration over being a counselor finally admitted that he just didn't seem to be able to help people with the same effectiveness he saw in colleagues he respected. In this case he felt guilt but not because he was wrong or right in the sense of sinful. He needed practical help. He required aid in the use of toys with small children and in developing greater listening powers with adults. He eventually learned how much therapy revolves around a relationship, not only a technique. As he developed into a good therapist, he liked his work and his anger diminished. Many people who feel angry at work would lose that anger if someone would take the time to help them do the job well. Even in school most of us hated classes we didn't understand and liked classes in which we excelled. I received a D- in high-school algebra and hated math. I earned an A in college algebra and decided that math was fascinating!

At times people feel anger in a job because they allow themselves to be walked over. Such a problem can occur at any level of employment. A top executive in a company sought counseling because he felt a total inability to delegate authority. Consequently he stayed in his office until nine or ten at night. It was difficult for him to correct the problem because he feared rejection from those he would have to confront. Yet as he slowly forced those under him to do their jobs, they began to respect him. In turn his self-esteem went up and his anger decreased.

There are times when it is not easy to avoid being walked over, especially if your position is subordinate, but even then there are ways to handle anger. A woman who sold greeting cards in a large department store was continually forced to endure the pickiness of her supervisor, a woman with many home problems she took out on people at work. At times the saleslady wanted to quit, but since she was single and untrained, leaving her job was not a valid option. In talking to her friends about the problem, she began to see the pathology of her supervisor. When she realized the problem did not reflect her own personal inadequacy, it became easier to ignore the supervisor's remarks.

There are times in a job or in other interpersonal relationships when anger takes over and stays and a state of resentment sets in. Especially at these times God enters the picture, for there is a love and a forgiveness only Christ can give. When I was very new in a job and very young, I worked under a supervisor who treated me and a number of other people unfairly. I was a teacher, and this woman only visited one of my classes. The majority of the students in that class spent their weekends in jail, and when I was absent from school, the substitute required administration protection. The supervisor never observed my well-behaved, advanced classes, and so my teacher ratings were low. At a certain point in the relationship, I became absolutely furious and considered quitting. I might have fought her by going over her head, but in either case I risked hurting my career. Ultimately I found my only peace in simply giving the person, myself, and my career to God in a new, more complete way. I can still remember the prayer: "Dear God, you know how I hate this woman. You know I'd only be playing games with you if I even said I want to like her. I don't. I thoroughly enjoy hating her, but I can't be close to you and hold on to hate. So because of that, I give you the right to love her through me. I ask you for a love I don't have and can't produce." Then my part of the responsibility was to *act* in love toward her; God's part was to give me the feelings—which didn't come all at once.

I began to eat lunch with her, ask about her family, smile when we encountered each other. I didn't like doing this, but I felt under God's command. Then the feelings came. I learned to genuinely *like* her although I always knew it was not wise to *trust* her. There's a difference. She had shown herself to be changeable, unpredictable, and untrustworthy. Yet it was a remarkable experience for me to see God loving her through me and to feel the absence of anger. The extra in this situation was when, apart from my intervention, her superiors saw me teach. Unknown to me at that time, they overrode her rating and gave me a superior mark. God only acted in that way after things were made right between him and me.

Perhaps above all, anger does not need to destroy us, even in a job where we are forced to spend one-third of our lives. Anger can motivate, overcome, and be transformed by the love and power of God.

Amy Carmichael says:

> No vision of the night can show, no word declare, with what longings of love Divine Love waits until the heart, all weary and sick of itself, turns to its Lord and says, "Take full possession." There is no need to plead that the love of God shall fill our heart as though He were unwilling to fill us: He is willing as light is willing to flood a room that is opened to its brightness, willing as water is willing to flow into an emptied channel. . . .

The words "grace for grace" have been a help to me since I read in a little old book of Bishop Moule's something that opened their meaning. (Till then I had not understood them.)

He says "for" means simply *instead:* "The image is of a perpetual succession of supply; a displacement ever going on; ceaseless changes of need and demand."

The picture before us is as of a river. Stand on its banks, and contemplate the flow of waters. A minute passes, and another. Is it the same stream still? Yes, but is it the same water? No. The liquid mass that passed you a few seconds ago fills now another section of the channel; new water has displaced it, or if you please replaced it; *water instead of water.* And so hour by hour, and year by year, and century by century, the process holds; one stream, other waters, living, not stagnant, because always in the great identity there is perpetual exchange. Grace takes the place of grace and love takes the place of love; ever new, ever old, ever the same, ever fresh and young, for hour by hour, for year by year, through Christ.[3]

In a world where we can do much to effect change through psychological understanding, we are ultimately dependent upon God for all we can do and become. When it comes to replacing anger with love, it is still the image of the river: "water instead of water . . . love takes the place of love."[4]

NOTES

1. Alvin Toffler, *Future Shock* (New York: Random House, 1970), p. 379.

2. Paul Tournier, *Guilt and Grace* (New York: Harper & Row, 1962), p. 94.

3. Amy Carmichael, *"If"* (Los Angeles, Cal.: Cowman Publications), p. 81.

4. Ibid.

6

Stored-Up Anger: Depression

It was the day after my father's funeral, and I had decided to go to a friend's home and relax for two days before resuming my work. I was experiencing that mixture of emotions so many people feel after the funeral of a loved one—a vague sense of disorientation as though everything had happened too fast to be real. Memories flooded my mind at every turn—the last time we went to the beach, the last dinner we had at this or that restaurant, indeed, the last anything we had shared. But there was also relief that the grossness of funeral preparations were over and that I no longer needed to hover in the somber atmosphere of the intensive care unit where my father had fought to live for five weeks. Basically, it was all over now. He was with the Lord. I needed to put my feet on the ground and live normally again.

My friend and I ate a late breakfast and then went out to wander through a couple of stores. It was good to look at life again and to buy trivia like make-up and a cheap gold chain. Yet even in the stores life seemed unwilling just to be normal, whatever "normal" is. The clerk told us about her fifteen-year-old nephew who had almost died in a recent automobile accident. Even then, since my friend seemed to be handling the clerk with an appropriate amount of sympathy, my mind wandered, and I caught myself watching a young, rather attractive woman nervously finger various bottles of nail polish.

When my friend turned and saw me watching the woman, she walked over to her and said hello. Apparently they were not close friends but had known each other on a PTA committee. Tears flooded the woman's eyes, and she told of her recent divorce. The haunted look on her face coupled with the poignant apathy with which she viewed life bothered my friend and me as we left the store and went home.

Later in the afternoon, still concerned, we called Connie's home. No answer. Since the minister of her church was the closest geographically to her house, we called him. He arrived in time to find Connie barely breathing after an overdose of sleeping pills.

Connie lived, but the depression persisted in full force, and she started counseling sessions. As is so typical, everyone offered advice. "Just forget your husband." "Date someone new." "Pray, don't you know this is all of Satan?" "You don't need counseling, you need to confess the sin of depression." And so went the wisdom of well-meaning, misguided friends who made a difficult problem more difficult.

Connie received some help from orthomolecular psychiatry, for bodily imbalances are often involved in depression. She received much assistance from Christians who built her up spiritually while recognizing her emotional needs. In our counseling sessions Connie came to face the low opinion she had of herself and succeeded in raising that self-image. She learned she was a very angry woman who had turned that anger in at herself in self-destructive rage.

Facing anger became important in Connie's recovery. Instead of submerging anger in destructive self-hatred, she began to be angry at the pain she was going through, and she determined to overcome it. Indicative of her increased self-esteem and thus her ability to turn depression into positive anger were statements like "I'm worth more than all this pain" and "There's no way a bad marriage is going to destroy my life." Of course, the determination fluctuated. Anger came and went, and at times Connie became deeply depressed again. But growing to like herself well enough to *use* anger, along with medical and spiritual support, was a vital key to her becoming the vibrant, happy person she is today.

Psychiatrist Rollo May speaks of those who have lost all self-respect, who have, as he puts it, given up their freedom. In them, says Dr. May, hatred smolders and may express itself in a myriad of symptoms.

Speaking of a potential positive aspect of anger, in contrast to depression and suicide, Dr. May says:

> Hating or resenting is often the person's only way to keep from committing psychological or spiritual suicide. It has the function of preserving some dignity, some feeling of his own identity, as though the person—or persons, in the case of nations—were to be saying silently to their conquerors, "You have conquered me, but I reserve the right to hate you." In cases of severe neurotics or psychotics, it is often exceedingly clear that the person, driven to the wall by earlier unfortunate conditions, has kept in his hatred an inner citadel, a last vestige of dignity and pride. Like the Negro in Faulkner's novel, *Intruder in the Dust,* such contempt for the conquerors keeps the person still an identity in his own right even though outward conditions deny him the essential rights of the human being.

In cases in therapy, furthermore, where a person who has been drastically curtailed in the exercise of his powers as a human being is unable, after a period of time, to feel or bring out his hatred and resentment, prognosis is less good. Just as the capacity of the little child to stand over against his parents was essential to his being born as a free person, so the harmed person's capacity eventually to hate or feel anger is a mark of his inner potentialities for standing against his oppressors. . . .

We of course do not mean that hatred or resentment in themselves are good things, or that the mark of the healthy person is how much he hates. . . . But the fact that the human being will destroy something—generally in the long run himself—rather than surrender his freedom proves how important freedom is to him.[1]

Dr. May's definition of freedom seems similar to what we mean by a good self-image, a sense of being, an identity. Attack on this identity brings anger which can be turned outward in the destructive act of the political assassin or turned inward into physical illness or depression or which can be channeled toward regaining the identity one has lost. Connie had lost her sense of being a person of worth and value; submerged within her, anger finally motivated her suicide attempt. Later, that same anger, expressed and accepted, motivated her to regain a state of sound mental health.

John, a boy of seventeen who was spaced out on drugs most of the time, became angry when his father shouted, "You'll never make anything out of yourself!" Instead of getting loaded that night, John studied to prove he could indeed be somebody. Some of his friends had been equally challenged by angry parental remarks and had passively slipped deeper into their world of drugs, in essence saying, "You've said I won't make it, so why should I try." Anger can destroy, but it can also challenge.

Anger and depression are among the most common problems of those who seek professional counseling. Furthermore, they are not new problems. Throughout biblical history great men of God labored under these two emotions, which are related even in the Scriptures. Jonah is perhaps the classic example. He was sent by God to warn the people of Nineveh about their sinfulness. This task he completed successfully to the point where the king of Nineveh turned from his sin and commanded his people to do likewise. In turn God "abandoned his plan to destroy them, and didn't carry it through" (Jon. 3:10, LB).

The biblical record goes on to say:

This change of plans made Jonah very angry. He complained to the Lord about it: "This is exactly what I thought you'd do, Lord, when I was there in my own country and you first told me to come here. . . . For I knew you were a gracious God, merciful, slow to get angry, and full of kindness; I knew how easily you could cancel your plans for destroying these people.

"Please kill me, Lord; I'd rather be dead than alive . . ."

Then the Lord said, "Is it right to be *angry* about *this?*"

So Jonah went out and sat sulking on the east side of the city (Jon. 4:1–5, LB).

However, all does not go well with Jonah; depressed, he sits under a vine. The vine dries, and the heat from the sun becomes intense. Then in a last recorded dialogue with God, Jonah states, "It is right for me to be angry enough to die" (Jon. 4:9, LB). Anger turned outward made Jonah desire Nineveh's destruction. Then he sought the cooling comfort of the vine, and his anger turned inward and became depression. At one point Jonah was content just to sit and "hole up," and at another point he wished for, indeed asked for, death.

While depression and anger are not usually linked this clearly in Scripture, they are presented as acceptable emotions when handled responsibly.

Secular literature abounds with thoughts of depression. Some of the most vivid illustrations of these feelings were written by those who lived in the last century. The economic and social turmoil of the Industrial Revolution and the intellectual trauma induced by scientific writers such as Charles Darwin prompted James Thomson, known as the poet of despair, to write with a feeling of relief, "This little life is all we must endure." Edward FitzGerald depressively stated, "I Myself am Heav'n and Hell."

While anger may be channeled so that it is helpful in overcoming depression, anger alone does not solve the deep existential vaccum. Thus during the stress in England in the late 1800s William Henley could at best, without God, survive by lashing out at life in his famous poem "Invictus."

Out of the night that covers me,
  Black as the Pit from pole to pole,
I thank whatever gods may be
  For my unconquerable soul.

In the fell clutch of circumstance
  I have not winced nor cried aloud.
Under the bludgeonings of chance
  My head is bloody, but unbowed.

Beyond this place of wrath and tears
  Looms but the horror of the shade,
And yet the menace of the years
  Finds, and shall find, me unafraid.

It matters not how strait the gate,
  How charged with punishments the scroll,
I am the master of my fate:
  I am the captain of my soul.

To meet the need for meaning that exists in all of us, Robert
Browning went beyond the anger of many writers of his time.
In an age of disillusionment Browning could say in faith:

. . . the acknowledgement of God in Christ
Accepted by thy reason, solves for thee
all questions in the earth and out of it *

We too live in an age of disillusionment. The church has failed
in the eyes of many. Explains Dr. Tournier:

. . . modern man appears to be disgusted with the religion
for which he nevertheless feels a homesickness. He has repressed it, banished it from his life, proclaimed the exclusion
of everything beyond the reach of the senses. He has consum-
mated a great rift between the spiritual and the temporal
world. And ever since, he has lived in a tragic duality.
  The great schism in man's life manifests itself in two
streams: the despiritualization of the world, on the one hand,
and the disincarnation of the church, on the other. At the
very time when the world wished to emancipate itself cultur-
ally and ethically from all moral or transcendent rules, the
church withdrew within itself and lost its sense of reality. It

talks about theology and psychology, feelings and doctrines, but no longer helps men in their real difficulties, of which it remains ignorant. It has fled into piety, into merely preaching salvation. Far be it from me to suggest that this is not its essential mission. But God also created the material world, not only the spiritual world. And the salvation he brings to us in Jesus Christ is not only the answer to the religious struggle of our souls, but also to the physical sufferings of the world. The language of the world and the language of the church have gone their separate ways, both with respect to content and to style. Magnificent sermons are preached in the church but the mass of men no longer come to hear them. They think the sermons are intended for the specialists who are preoccupied with theology. They do not expect from them anything that will contribute to the solution of the real problems of social, economic, and cultural life with which they have to grapple. Ministers—I know less about the Catholic church, but I suppose the priests also—appear to most men of our time to be idealists who have little understanding of practical life, who in any case cover up with pious phrases the cultural and social problems, the technical complexity of which they are quite unaware. "The church," a patient recently said to me, "stands outside of history."[2]

Marty, a twenty-year-old predental student in a large university, found the organized church far outside the history of her life, and today she is dead.

Suffering from a form of mental illness now controllable by medication, Marty went through the tortures of the damned and tried to die. Medical science came through and saved her life after the first suicide attempt. I was young at the time, probably nineteen, and knew Marty only briefly. A friend and I talked to her. We called a local church; they were too busy even to put the phone call through to the minister. We called a Christian friend; she thought it was hopeless and didn't even try to see her although Marty had requested such a visit. The church community around us at that time had truly "fled into piety," and Marty, in her apartment, hung herself. The sense of loss of a girl who had straight A's even when she couldn't go to class overwhelmed me and became one of my most bleak college memories. If love could have made her live then, medication more recently discovered could save her now.

Sometimes the local church can be brought back to life much as doctors stimulate a cardiac arrest by using electric shock. Recently, a crippled polio victim of twenty had no one to help her at home and no one to drive her to church. Again, I hopefully called a church to see if anyone had time to do something; the girl needed more than what I or my friends were already doing.

"Is she a church member?" the secretary asked.

"No," I answered.

"Then we can't help," she explained. "We only help members."

"But that's the point," I protested. "She can't *get* to church."

"Sorry, we only help members," she repeated. "If not, we'd be overwhelmed."

Losing my cool, I coldly replied, "She *is* a member of the body of Christ!"

There was a dead silence. Then, "I'll have the pastor call you." He never did!

But two weeks later fourteen teenagers heard about the situation through the church and visited the girl. They fixed her house, outside and in, cooked, drove her to the doctor, and took her to church. The organized church failed, but, thank God, certain members of the body of Christ remembered that in that body "If one part suffers, all parts suffer with it, and if one part is honored, all the parts are glad" (1 Cor. 12:26, LB).

At the same time in our society, family units hardly exist. Many teenagers who see me professionally have numerous stepbrothers and sisters and even several parents. They feel rootless, belonging to everyone and no one. They are disciplined by two fathers and loved occasionally by both. Adults are in no better a condition. Married, many live with a sense of impermanence about whether those who love them today will stay around tomorrow. Fortunately, Christianity stabilizes and helps cement relationships; yet Christian marriages and families are far from immune to the same insecurities. Indeed, sometimes the only difference is that because of their convictions and guilt they are more willing to live in hell on earth a little longer than the average. Please do not misunderstand. Such conditions among Christians are not an indictment of Christianity but an indictment of our relationship with God.

Furthermore science, which thirty years ago promised everything but immortality, seems to be helpless to make a person happy, much less immortal. We, like Henley and other nineteenth-century writers, can look at our century and ask, "For what are we suffering all this pain?" More people in the world go to bed hungry than full. More marriages fail than succeed. Disaster from pollution, overpopulation, or starvation is an imminent reality. While expressing and channeling anger will alleviate some depression, ultimately one must seek comfort and release in the spiritual dimension.

Joseph Fabry, who espouses Frankl's logotherapy approach, states that "a psychiatrist is required to make a diagnosis based on the *totality* of the patient. . . . mental disease may originate in the patient's body (caused by the malfunctioning of a gland, for instance), his psyche (caused, for example, by a childhood trauma), or his noös (caused, perhaps, by a value conflict)."[3]

Fabry goes on to cite an example of a school teacher suffering from depression caused by all three areas—spiritual, psychological, and physical. Dealing with anger in her case would have helped only part of the problem. Her depression was:

> . . . diagnosed as being caused organically, and an appropriate drug was prescribed. But the depression also had a psychological cause: she was depressed over her depressions; her immediate condition was but a psychological reaction to something that originally had been an organic defect. In therapeutic sessions she was instructed to avoid brooding as much as possible because such brooding would understandably but

unjustifiably magnify her bleak views. Frankl suggested to her to let the depression pass by her as the cloud passes the sun: the sun exists behind the cloud even if we cannot see it for the moment. Such therapy released much that was unlocked in the patient, but also disclosed her existential distress: her low opinion of herself as a person whom fate had hopelessly handicapped with recurring depressions. Here logotherapy in the strict sense of the word was indicated. Frankl convinced her that what matters is the attitude people take toward their unchangeable fate, that her depressions posed a challenge for her. She could decide to shape her life in spite of the difficulties that had developed. In time the patient learned to see her life as full of personal tasks, in spite of the depressions. Indeed, the depressions presented an additional task: that of living with them, of overcoming them instead of being crushed by them. The patient led a life "more conscious of responsibility and more filled with meaning than before treatment—more so, probably, than if she had never fallen ill and never needed treatment." She later wrote Frankl, "I was not a human being until you made me one," which prompted him to recall a sentence by Goethe, "If we take people as they are, we make them worse. If we treat them as if they were what they ought to be, we help them become what they are capable of becoming." Frankl considers this sentence "the finest maxim for any kind of psychotherapy."[4]

While Frankl's patient undoubtedly had aspects of anger in this depression in which she felt inadequate and defeated, she also lacked meaning because of the depression. Once again the Christian message has an answer that psychology and medicine cannot give.

A patient of mine who was severely suicidal but who had no diagnosable organic basis for this tendency became a Christian. The thought that the psalmist expressed regarding God, "How precious it is, Lord, to realize that you are thinking about me constantly" (Ps. 139:17, LB), struck this woman with great force on both a psychological and a spiritual level. After conversion, her life's purpose was pleasing God, Frankl's idea of serving one's "Taskmaster," and psychologically she felt worth because

God loved her. In a miraculously short time she was well enough to quit therapy. Because she was never deeply depressed after her conversion and because she had been in therapy only two or three weeks prior to conversion, we professionals involved had to admit we had not performed the cure. God had. God does not always work that quickly and thoroughly, but he can and in this case he did. The greatest of all God's saints have variously experienced instant healing, progressive healing, partial healing, and no healing. God will not be limited to our methods, timing, and desires. He remains unpredictable which becomes part of our definition of him, for if we could predict him, he would cease to be God or we would be divine.

Nor can the physical be overlooked. Illness of any kind brings anger and depression. Certain physical disorders such as hypoglycemia (low blood sugar) and thyroid malfunctioning can directly cause depression. Vitamins, minerals, and diet are also vital in maintaining emotional balance. Dr. Harvey Ross, an orthomolecular psychiatrist in Los Angeles, has had remarkable success in treating depression. He says:

> . . . There are many effective psychiatric treatments. It is the duty of the psychiatrist to know these treatments and to prescribe the right treatment for the patient who consults him as an expert in mental health. Shock treatment is not a good treatment for every psychiatric patient. Psychotherapy is not a good treatment for every psychiatric patient. Vitamins are not the sole answer to many psychiatric problems. But as psychiatrists we must know what treatment may be useful and when to use it. We must stop holding to any narrow viewpoint as the answer to all psychiatric problems. The field of psychiatry has grown tremendously and rapidly. It is time that we as psychiatrists do the same.
>
> In my experience as an orthomolecular psychiatrist, I find that many patients who complain of depression have hypoglycemia (low blood sugar). Because hypoglycemia is, in my opinion, so prevalent and causes so much misery and is so misunderstood, I feel it is mandatory to consider the possibility of this disorder whenever a patient complains of depres-

sion. Hypoglycemia may be a contributing factor to the depression, and, in some cases, it may be the total cause.[5]

Moreover, if an illness is of a long duration, anger becomes a strong factor which is difficult for the healthy to understand. This is partly explainable by Tournier's description of the ill:

> . . . One always feels rather guilty at arousing revulsion in others, at causing, by illness, a disturbance in the family, an extra burden of work for one's colleagues at the office, extra work and worry for one's wife. Thus a majority of sick people at first refuse to admit that they are ill, they refuse to go to bed or to consult the doctor. All this false guilt about illness is a very common cause of culpable self-neglect.[6]

Psychiatrist E. B. Mohns of Scripps Clinic in La Jolla, California, has been involved in that institution's Pain Treatment Center which attempts to help people who suffer from chronic, incurable pain. Furthermore in other aspects of his research Dr. Mohns has dealt extensively with the emotions of those who are ill and will never be well. He says there is "some degree of psychological difficulty commensurate with their pain. The experience of chronic pain will make you mad at yourself, mad at the people around you, mad specifically at the physicians who have failed to obliterate the pain. The anger is ineffective. Then fatigue becomes a component just due to the experience of chronic pain and the limitation of life style. Then the more obvious depression component comes in."

Dr. Mohns agrees that this depression comes from anger which is turned inward and also from the sheer stress of chronic pain. He says that patients with terminal illnesses are enraged at their bodies for betraying them and enraged at whatever they may have done to contribute to their illness. Characteristically they find the need for sporadic periods of mourning over the part of self they are losing. They anticipate that time when they may be helpless, disgusting, stink, and lose bladder and bowel functions. They fear the shame connected with this.

Practical answers are not easy, quick, or obvious. Dr. Mohns believes that people need to ventilate their anger, particularly at the physician whom they feel has failed them. He feels the appropriate response from the physician is to ask, "What are you going to do about it?"

Says Dr. Mohns, "The main way that you know you're alive, sick or well, is by the moment to moment awareness you have of your being able to have impact on the environment in some meaningful way and getting feedback from the environment that you exist. One way of dealing with anger and depression is to behaviorally insist that the chronically ill do things, basically of an assertive nature which tends to deal with both anger and depression."

An example which Dr. Mohns gave in his interview was of the political mileage made by the Pulmonary Association in terms of getting segments of public places set aside for non-smokers. Someone with advanced emphysema, for example, could then eat dinner and not start gagging and turn blue because of a big cigar in the next booth.

In my practice patients who hurt express anger and depression over their helplessness to control their bodies and environment and over what they feel is rejection from friends who find them "a drag" or who feel they should "get a grip on their emotions." "Don't let it get you down" or "Just think of how many people are worse off than you" are common, irritating statements.

C. S. Lewis states that "pain provides an opportunity for heroism; the opportunity is seized with surprising frequency." Somehow depression, when it can be changed into anger and focused on a task or goal, helps many toward such heroism.

A young girl crippled from an automobile accident said to me, "My worst handicap is not physical; it's emotional. If I could just fight to handle these physical problems, I'd make it, but right now I feel so depressed."

On October 6, 1802, Ludwig van Beethoven wrote a striking

letter to his brothers. In part it dealt with his struggle over years of total deafness. Yet during that time Beethoven wrote his greatest musical compositions. In part the letter reads:

> O you men who consider, or describe me as quarrelsome, peevish or misanthropic, how greatly you wrong me! You do not know the secret reason why I seem to you to be so. From my childhood onward my heart and soul have been filled with tender feelings of goodwill, and I have always been willing to perform great and magnanimous deeds. But reflect, for the past 6 years I have been in an incurable condition made worse by unreasonable doctors. From year to year I have hoped to be cured, but in vain, and at last I have been forced to accept the prospect of a permanent infirmity. . . . I soon had to cut myself off and live in solitude. When, occasionally, I decided to ignore my infirmity, ah, how cruelly I was then driven back by the doubly sad experience of my poor hearing, yet I could not find it in myself to say to people: "Speak louder, shout, for I am deaf." Ah, how could I possibly have referred to the weakening of a sense which ought to be more perfectly developed in me than in other people. . . . Sometimes I have been driven by my desire to seek the company of other human beings, but what humiliation when someone, standing beside me, heard a flute from afar off while I heard nothing. . . . Such experiences have brought me close to despair, and I came near to ending own life—only my art held me back, as it seemed to me impossible to leave this world until I have produced everything I feel it has been granted to me to achieve.[7]

Despair, anger, attempts to achieve, and truly great achievement were the results of Beethoven's chronic illness; yet he lived with constant pain, in his words a "miserable existence," for pain is not only confined to physical torture but also to the anguish of the emotions. In spite of his pain, Beethoven made an "impact on the environment in some meaningful way," and his environment has not ceased to give feedback that he did truly exist. Apparently his depression and anger were deep, but perhaps because of them he determiend to go on; in Frankl's terminology he found the way for his existence, a meaning deep enough to keep him alive.

We Americans with our fast answers—marathon therapy sessions, pills for every psychic twinge, and even easy, facile spiritualizations of problems—have developed a shallowness in our approach to pain and its resultant depression. A Catholic nun suffering from physically induced depression presents the problem more realistically in her diary:

> For, a person who assumes that his life must consist of stepping from success to success is like a fool who stands next to a building site and shakes his head because he cannot understand why people dig deep down when they set out to build a cathedral. God builds a temple out of each man's soul, and in my case He is just starting out to excavate the foundations. It is my task to offer myself to His excavations.[8]

Suffering accepted and embraced as desirable is masochistic. Suffering which is unavoidable and in which there develops spiritual meaning and psychological growth marks greatness in a person. Often, anger is a vital tool in developing that greatness.

Unfortunately within society in general and particularly within the Christian community depression is stigmatized as sinful and indicative of weakness and spiritual inadequacy. Nevertheless, Charles Spurgeon, the great nineteenth-century preacher, saw depression as far from sinful although painful. Says one of his biographers, Richard Day:

> There was one aspect of Spurgeon's life, glossed over by most of his biographers, that we must now view with utter frankness—he was frequently in the grip of terrific depression moods. This offers no difficulty whatever to any Christian who does sometimes himself walk the floor of hell, on and on, until he finds a Hand that brings him out. The sweetness of his release giveth him such radiant new love for his Redeemer, that he doth then find in his head the tongue of the taught, enabling him to sustain with words any other that may be weary. The function of "word sustention" is the chief part of Christian ministry. That Saint of Neuritis, Dr. J. H. Jowett, said, "The world wants to be comforted." *He knew that;* and he knew wondrously well how it is done. The

tongue of the taught belongs only to those who also are men of sorrows and acquainted with grief.[9]

Spurgeon suffered recurrent physical problems from his early teens. Often these difficulties interfered with his ministry.

The storm of affliction broke into a steady roar after his forty-third year, necessitating his making almost twenty fall-winter trips to the sunshine of Mentone, France. This took him out of his pulpit two or three of the most valuable months of the year. Under such constraint his spirit chafed: "We *could* do more, we *would* do more, if we were not laid prostrate at the very moment our work requires our presence. Therefore, while we live, every interval of relief shall be laid out in his service. The time is short, the work is great, the Lord must be trusted more simply." Once his depression grew to such size, that he intimated resigning. But his officiary said, "We would rather have you one month in the year than any other twelve."[10]

Yet this very humanness was used to uplift others. A letter from a parishioner showed this quality.

Oh, Mr. Spurgeon, that little word of yours, "I am feeling low," struck a chord which still vibrates in my spirit. It was to me like reading the Forty-second Psalm. I imagine there is nothing in your ministry to the saints that comes home more tenderly to tried and stricken souls than just what you there express, "I am feeling low." The great preacher, the author of *The Treasury of David*, this man sometimes, aye, often, "feels low" just as they do. In all their affliction he was afflicted—this is what draws hearts to Jesus; and the principle is just the same when the friends and intimates of Jesus "feel low." The fellow feeling, thus begotten, makes many wondrous kind.
Your friend in Jesus,
JOHN LOUSON.[11]

Elsewhere Spurgeon describes some of the times when depression most often occurs for all of us:

The times most favorable to fits of depression, so far as I have experienced, may be summed up in a brief catalogue.

First among them I mention *the hour of great success.* When at last a long-cherished desire is fulfilled, when God has been glorified greatly by our means, a great triumph achieved, then we are apt to faint. . . .

Before any great achievement, some measure of the same depression is very usual. Surveying the difficulties before us, our hearts sink within us. . . . This depression comes over me whenever the Lord is preparing a larger blessing for my ministry. . . .

In the midst of a long stretch of unbroken labour, the same affliction may be looked for. The bow cannot be always bent without fear of breaking. Repose is as needful to the mind as sleep to the body. . . .

This evil will also come upon us, we know not why, and then it is all the more difficult to drive it away. Causeless depression is not to be reasoned with. . . . If those who laugh at such melancholy did but feel the grief of it for one hour, their laughter would be sobered into compassion. . . .

If it be inquired why the valley of the shadow of death must so often be traversed by the servants of King Jesus, the answer is not far to find. All this is promotive of the Lord's mode of working, which is summed up in these words: "Not by might nor by power, but my Spirit, saith the Lord. . . . Heaven shall be all the fuller of bliss because we have been filled with anguish here below, and earth shall be better tilled because of our training in the school of adversity.[12]

Certainly Spurgeon's words speak of anything but stigma. Rather they encourage depressed persons to know they may be molded into special instruments for God's service. Depression may not be something any of us would seek, but it is an emotion that can be used rather than wasted. Of all things in this world worse than suffering, wasted suffering is certainly high on the list.

While we may understand and accept depression, it is not pleasant, and we need to learn practical ways to handle it. Holing up in one's house or room is about the most destructive thing a depressed person can do, for it fosters depression. As one teenager said, "I'm awfully depressed; so I guess I'd better not stay home and read tomorrow. I'd better stay active." A suicidal patient needed my daily telephone call to challenge her even to get dressed or go to the grocery store, but she responded, and today she is a happy, fairly well-adjusted person.

Depressed people usually want to withdraw from others' company, but what they need most is positive feedback from people which says "You're okay" or "I like you." Furthermore, people offer diversion, sometimes a way to break a depressive cycle.

At times physical exercise can be helpful in getting rid of angry, depressive feelings, at least temporarily. Speaking of himself, Dr. Mohns says:

Many days I come home tired and I feel like I've been beaten with clubs, phones ringing off the wall all day and doing this and that. Clearly I'm angry. And then I go running and then I feel well. I feel rested. It's not that I'm angry at the patients or at the doctors. It's just a matter of the pace, but self-chosen.

For myself, swimming hard helps release the tension of anger and reduce depression. However, such temporary methods are appropriate for mild or periodic depression. They do not aid in removing deep-seated or long-range causes of depression and anger.

In his excellent book *Love Yourself,* Walter Trobisch says:

In a way each person is his own best doctor when it comes to curing depression. I know a lady who often suffers from depression with no apparent outward cause. When she is in this state it prohibits her from thinking clearly and acting objectively, so she had made for herself what she calls a "depression emergency kit." Like a doctor's prescription, she has written down instructions to herself telling her what to do in case of a depression. First of all, she has a little box of cards with special Bible verses containing promises and assurances. She picks out a card and reads it aloud. Next, she makes herself a good cup of tea which she sips slowly while listening to a favorite record. She also has on hand an absorbing book which she has been burning to read but which she has saved for this occasion. Afterward she calls up a friend and combines the visit to her with a walk in the fresh air.[13]

I know women who have their hair done differently and men who buy a new garden tool when they feel down.

Yet for deep, angry depression simple answers do not always work, and a process of time and even professional help may be required. For those who experience such depression there is the knowledge that what they are suffering is not uncommon, that their pain does not make lesser persons out of them, and that the depression can be relieved even if it *feels* as if it could never be assuaged. Anger is one important tool in this relief as are drugs (usually on a temporary basis), vitamin therapy, diet control, and the divine touch God gives in his time and through his instruments.

> Yet in the middle of the pain there is a place where . . . we encounter God, in which we are held by God. This experience gives us the courage to love ourselves *with* our depressions and be cheerful even with a heavy heart. It reflects a depth of faith which the Apostle Paul expressed with the paradoxical statement: "As servants of God we commend ourselves in every way . . . as *sorrowful, yet always* rejoicing' " (2 Cor. 6:4, 10, RSV).[14]

NOTES

1. Rollo May, *Man's Search for Himself* (New York: W. W. Norton, 1953), pp. 149–51.

2. Paul Tournier, *The Whole Person in a Broken World* (New York: Harper & Row, 1964), pp. 78–79.

3. Joseph B. Fabry, *The Pursuit of Meaning* (Boston: Beacon Press, 1968), p. 152.

4. Ibid., pp. 153–54.

5. Harvey Ross, *Fighting Depression* (New York: Larchmont Books, 1975), pp. 75–77.

6. Paul Tournier, *Guilt and Grace* (New York: Harper & Row, 1962), p. 20.

7. Ludwig van Beethoven, *The Heiligenstadt Testament,* ed. Joseph Schmidt and Gorg and Hans Schmidt (Hamburg: Polydoe International, 1974, Bicentennial Edition 1770–1970), p. 21.

8. Fabry, *Pursuit of Meaning,* p. 48.

9. Richard Ellsworth Day, *The Shadow of the Broad Brim* (Philadelphia: Judson Press, 1934), p. 173.

10. Ibid., p. 175.

11. Ibid., p. 179.

12. Helmut Thielicke, *Encounter with Spurgeon* (Grand Rapids: Baker Book House, 1975 reprint), pp. 218–23.

13. Walter Trobisch, *Love Yourself* (Downers Grove: Inter-Varsity Press, 1976), p. 46.

14. Ibid., p. 53.

7

Creative Anger

At the back window of her bedroom, Reneé stood straight, almost frozen, staring out over the lovely green lawn of her backyard. It was ten in the morning. I entered the room quietly, having let myself in after no one answered the doorbell. A half-hour earlier Renée had hysterically begged me to come over quickly. Not knowing any details, I came, hair still in rollers, dressed in jeans and a sloppy T-shirt—not at all my idea of getting dressed to go out although good enough for the day I had planned at home, writing and bathing the dog.

As I looked at Renée's expensive dressing gown, well-groomed blow-dry hair style, and perfect house, I wondered why on earth I was standing there waiting for this friend of a friend, whom I hardly knew, to acknowledge my presence and tell me what was wrong.

She finally turned toward me, and it was obvious she had been crying for a long time. She shook violently, and her face went white in a fresh burst of tears. When at length the weeping subsided, she began to talk. For years her marriage had been bad, but she had endured it, mainly for social reasons and because she was unsure of whether her religious convictions would allow her to consider divorce. Three or four times she had reached the end, had become hysterical, and had required the assistance of a friend. Once she had to be sedated by a doctor.

At first her hysteria had seemed to be a reaction to the behavior of Ed, her husband. On a couple of occasions he had a few too many drinks and had hit her. Her extremely emotional response had frightened him into a more sensible pattern of behavior, but still the hysteria came. This morning Ed had forgotten to take out the trash before he went to work, and Renee had discovered it when she got up. Obviously Ed's omission in itself could not have precipitated the present crisis. It was merely the catalyst that brought out a lot of other bad feelings, culminating in an anger Renée did not understand or know how to express.

In very few counseling sessions Renée recognized that her shakiness and uncontrollable crying primarily manifested unfaced anger. She began to feel the anger directly and to express it appropriately. Since then, although her circumstances have not changed, she has, and her helpless crying episodes have been channeled into active life-changes. Whether or not the marriage will work, I do not know, but either way, Renee will make it. She has learned to use anger rather than be destroyed by it.

When a person becomes angry, his or her whole body is involved. We have all experienced the tight muscular tension, the shakiness, and the rapid heartbeat that come when anger is held in but not resolved. Our frustration lies in the conflict between the desire to act out angry impulses and the wish to keep them under control.

What we actually do with anger will be either destructive or constructive. The man who felt intense rage at his wife and in-laws but suppressed his feelings ended up in a hospital emergency room one night with bleeding ulcers. A little girl kept hitting her playmates at school because she was jealous over her newborn brother. An elderly lady snapped at all the nurses in the resthome where she lived until most of them refused to come near her unless caring for her essential needs. All these people were angry. They hurt themselves or others with their anger, and each handled his or her anger in a way which engendered more anger. The man with the ulcer blamed his family more when he got sick. The little girl became enraged because nobody would play with her at school. The elderly lady resented what became genuine neglect by the nurses. These are just a few of many possible destructive expressions of anger. Any behavior that irresponsibly hurts oneself or others either verbally or physically is destructive and for the Christian is wrong.

Apparently, modes of expressing anger constructively are hard to discover in our society. In my mail, for example, I receive dozens of brochures on assertiveness training seminars. I see numerous magazine articles on positive anger or how to make anger work for you. Evidently, we do have a problem with anger that we want very much to resolve.

Many people vent their anger by developing and using a stronger vocabulary than they ordinarily employ. However, such a vocabulary engenders guilt, it becomes a destructive release. For example, the Bible clearly teaches that the Christian is to avoid profanity. The use of it then would be destructive for a Christian.

A raised tone of voice and the use of unusual or so-called four-letter words are a way of releasing anger. Many people reserve such words for private expression, or they say them only in the presence of someone who will not be condemnatory. Apart from the moral issue (which is not important for discussion in this context), such a practice does seem to allow many people to get anger out rather than bottle it up or hurt others.

Most four-letter words currently in use relate to bodily functions. Some have sexual implications, but most concern the urinary or digestive tracts. They are effective expressions of anger in this society *only* because such bodily functions are considered private and at times dirty and nasty. In my practice I have seen small children urinate against a bedroom wall or smear fecal matter across furniture or woodwork. This was their ultimate weapon. They knew that these acts punished their parents far more than spilling food—or throwing it, for that matter—because we have a social aversion to these bodily functions. Four-letter words are perhaps the adult version of the overt activity of these children. Four-letter words shock, silence, and express depth of feeling. "Thus, for instance, everyone feels a special pleasure in using a well-placed slang or swearword. It is defiance hurled at the over-rigorous, crushing tutelage of good form, a healthy affirmation of independence in the face of social pressure."[1] People listen who didn't listen before, but of course, they may also reject the person who is venting feelings in this manner. Such a practice then becomes destructive for both the speaker and the hearer. Many of our four-letter words would have no shock effect in countries where bathroom-related subjects are casually accepted as part of everyday life. In parts of Europe the walls of outside public toilets extend only to a person's waist and are not designated for men or women. In parts of Asia there are no public toilets; the elimination process is considered natural enough to be done wherever the urge hits. I imagine that people of these countries would be confused or even amused by the elaborate designs shown in our home-improvement magazines—bathrooms with oversized tubs, running waterfalls, sun lamps, and a variety of toilets, to say nothing of growing plants, hanging candles, and elaborate color and lighting!

Yet each country has its shock subjects and shock words. Years ago a European man was directing a building project in China. Workmen were easy to get, and their financial expectations were minimal, but it was very difficult to get them to work together for any length of time. The European tried persuasion, bribery, threats. Nothing worked. Then he remembered a peculiarity he had heard about these people. Our four-letter words did not phase them, for what was shocking about a natural body process? Profanity also did not affect them, and besides, the European would have had his own guilt feelings about using profanity. But one thing did bother them—being called a "thing!" The worse, most despicable word one could apply to them was *thing*. It dehumanized them, made them less than people.

With a megaphone and a loud voice the European once again asked for the men's attention. Once again they paid little attention. Then he shouted in Chinese dialogue, "You thing you!" A deadening silence fell over the group and looks of anger crossed the men's faces. Slowly but deliberately they picked up their equipment and went to work. Offended and silent, they worked through the afternoon. He had been heard and his anger perceived.

"You thing you" would mean as little to an American as one of our four-letter words would have meant to those men in China. At best, the words would amuse, but because in these respective cultures they lack shock value, they would neither release nor create anger.

In observing angry people, I have noticed that the use of four-letter words is sometimes a barometer of a rising anger-level. True, some teenagers use these words continually, an indication that the words no longer mean much or that these young people have slumped into a sloppy means of communicating. Younger children occasionally parrot words they have heard but which for them have no meaning. One youngster kept calling everyone a "fag." When I finally asked him what the word meant, he didn't know. He was flabbergasted at its true meaning and stopped using the word so often. However, when the average person starts throwing out words that offend some and are not characteristic of his or her usual vocabulary, it is like waving a red flag to say, "I am angry. Hear me. Stop!"

Releasing anger verbally is an important way of dealing with hostile emotion, but it is certainly not restricted to or even dependent upon the use of four-letter words. Talking out angry feelings with a person who is safe, who will not repeat what is said, and who will care and understand can be a valuable safety valve. A friend who was weary of his sister-in-law's extended visit called me to gripe about his feelings. The sister-in-law was leaving in two days; Ed liked her and certainly loved his wife. Rather than hurt either of them by talking about a situation that would soon be resolved anyway, he got his feelings out by talking to me. It didn't hurt me; his family never found out his feelings which were only temporary; and Ed not only avoided a destructive bottling up of feelings but his behavior toward his visiting relative for the remaining two days of her visit was positive and genuine.

A man less verbally inclined than Ed, or Ed if he had been in a different mood, would perhaps have gone swimming or jogging. Some people release feelings by weeding a garden or cleaning house. Some physical activities loosen the tension that has built up in the muscles, and they refocus the mind on something not particularly demanding emotionally but exhausting physically.

When kids talk about getting their heads together, they have a point. It is sometimes helpful to remove oneself from an anger-producing situation and get a realistic perspective. Once when I was working at a clinic, I became angry over some personnel problems and the resultant effect on patients. I was close to walking out or blowing up, neither of which would have accomplished anything. For me the ocean is a never-failing escape. As I watch the waves, life takes on perspective. Breathing in the fresh salt air and feeling the wet wind hitting my face and blowing through my hair give me a sense of renewal. So, as usual, under this stress I headed for the beach, this time for dinner since it was late in the day. A friend and I sat for a long time looking out over the dark ocean and listening to the waves hit the shore, and I sorted out my angry feelings from the real issues involved.

Back at work the next day my anger had diminished into a calm determination to stand up for what I believed. What I believed was not now distorted by anger which had made me look at things disproportionately. I had gotten away from the source of my anger and that had helped.

There are many ways to handle and release anger, but the most productive is to *use* anger creatively. Certainly this method has deep historical significance in America. The motivation behind America's separation from England was anger over the indignities England had forced upon its colonies. You might well say that anger forced the birth of a new, independent nation. Indeed the Revolutionary War was fought as much with words as it was with artillery and force.

Thomas Paine spoke of that kind of anger in December 1776:

> I once felt all that kind of anger, which a man ought to feel, against the mean principles that are held by the Tories. A noted one, who kept a tavern at Amboy, was standing at his door, with as pretty a child in his hand, about eight or nine years old, as I ever saw, and after speaking his mind as freely as he thought was prudent, finished with this unfatherly expression, "Well! give me peace in my day." Not a man lives on the continent but fully believes that a separation must sometime or other finally take place, and a generous parent should have said, "If there must be trouble, let it be in my day, that my child may have peace;" and this single reflection, well applied, is sufficient to awaken every man to duty.[2]

Some of the verse of the times reflects the further influence of anger in fighting the British. An unknown poet illustrated the motivating frustration: "Old England's cruel tyranny induced him to go forth."

Had Great Britain never imposed unreasonable taxes, had she paid more respect to the colonists' voice in determining their own destiny, the colonies would have been content. But indignity heaped upon indignity moved early Americans to an anger that could not be extinguished and which found its resolution in the establishment of a new, independent country.

Creative anger can make the impossible seem possible. Months ago I visited an elderly friend at a convalescent home. It was located some distance from my home, and I had never been there before. As I drove into the parking lot, my first impression was positive. The building was attractive and well kept. It was a hot day, and so the cool waiting room was a pleasant relief from the soaring temperature outside. Then came the blow. In the patients' rooms there was no air conditioning, not even a fan. The body odor from people who had not recently bathed combined with the stench of urine and a stifling heat almost overcame me. I walked from room to room, and the farther I went, the worse conditions became. Dirt of all varieties was smeared across the curtains; bedspreads were torn; food had been left to flies and the decay of heat. One elderly lady who thought I had come to stay warned, "Get out now. This is a terrible place to be."

By the time I left, after making sufficient phone calls to insure my friend's transfer to another home, I was seething with an anger for which I could think of no constructive, appropriate outlet. I ranted to a few friends, but that didn't help. Finally I did something my normal cynical realism would not have permitted. I sat down and with articulate wrath wrote to a high-ranking governmental official. Of course, I thought my letter would never be read, at least by him, but it was something I had to do.

A few weeks later I received a personal reply from the man, with additional questions. Then another letter, then a phone call, then an investigation committee who went to the home and, I hope, forced some improvements. Apparently I had hit a political nerve ending. My anger had found a creative outlet, releasing me from my Fury as well as effecting some positive action.

Not all anger can become creative, but one should always look for positive potential. Anger at a political system can make one person run for office and another attempt to assassinate a political leader. Anger over child abuse can make a mother who was abused herself treat her own children cruelly or she can determine to be a different kind of parent. A deaf Beethoven could have spent his remaining days wallowing in anger and self-pity, or he could, as he did, write his best works.

Anger relates to self-esteem. The person who uses anger positively likes himself better; the person who hurts himself or others with his rage likes himself less. Depending on our level of self-esteem, we will be more or less prone to angry feelings. A person with a low self-image will be more sensitive to criticism, more touchy, more easily made angry. Within ourselves we change almost daily depending on how life is proceeding. When my life is smooth, I feel better about myself and am less likely to be easily provoked. But if everything on a given day has gone wrong, I may become irritable with little or no provocation. Only God really knows where we are inside, and his condemnation and reward for how we handle anger is bound up in how strong the temptation was for us at a given time. People judge us by our outward appearance. God judges us by our inward climate—what we feel about ourselves, how vulnerable we are to a given stimulus, how hard we try to react in a right way.

Cindy was a small, slight child of eight when I first met her. She had been through two years of frequent surgeries after an accident in which she had been badly burned. She was not pretty. Since birth she had worn a leg brace, and right now her teeth were also in braces. Her hair never seemed to go in the right direction, and she wore thick glasses. Her family kidded her about being a walking catastrophe, something she didn't find funny. She literally hated her pretty ten-year-old sister and her athletic, bright seven-year-old brother. Cindy was an angry child, and she had a right to be.

After two or three visits to me, she came in one day in a complete rage. A boy had tripped her on purpose, and she had failed a math test for which her mother had grounded her for the weekend. Grabbing and raising a stick from the pool game in my office, she shouted: "I hate everyone, even you." I didn't move. Slowly she lowered the stick away from me and began to sob. For Cindy, this was a big step forward. In spite of her deep-seated anger, she stopped herself from physically hurting me. She wanted to hurt someone, anyone, but she didn't. In God's sight, restraint in face of that deep a desire is far more commendable than the restraint of a person who is under comparative little temptation. After this incident, Cindy and I worked through a lot of her anger just by talking.

Certain groups of people in any society and those in certain stages of life have a more difficult time with anger because they feel less able to deal with it directly and positively. Children, the very ill, the mentally incompetent, and the aged fall into this category.

Basic to anger experienced in old age is the feeling of uselessness, of being in the way, of not being needed or wanted. Unfortunately, this attitude is so built into our culture it has become self-perpetuating. Old people are expected to be senile (a much-abused word), and people usually live out society's expectations. Being put down when you were once in control generates deep anger; yet if that anger bursts out in the form of complaints, the elderly person is termed cantankerous. If an old man stubbornly leaves a convalescent home where he didn't want to be in the first place, he is placed in restraints or put in a locked facility because "he doesn't know what he is doing." Thus his anger increases.

The problem is many-faceted and not easy to solve. Some elderly people need the care of a convalescent hospital because they cannot be medically cared for at home, because they have no home, or because they are difficult to manage and disturb and destroy the lives of their children or other relatives. One must be careful, however, not to use any of the above reasons as a cop-out for irresponsibility.

Whatever the cause and wherever elderly persons in this society find themselves, there is a good chance that they will feel useless, somewhat degraded, and therefore angry. Typically they have less money, poorer health, fewer friends, and less purpose. Until society changes, it is up to the elderly to handle their anger wisely.

One normal but elderly woman said, "I never thought my life would end with such strong feelings of hopelessness and loneliness." She had sold her home after her husband's death and had moved into a home for the aged. "In exchange for lifetime residency" she gave up all her assets—money from the house sale, life savings, and monthly Social Security check. She was allowed a few personal belongings and twenty dollars a month.

When she moved in, the first question she was asked was "Mrs. Mello, where do you intend to be buried?"

She was criticized for having a bookcase, a scatter rug, and drapes. The latter two made it difficult to clean—and who needed books?

She says, "I can still feel the anger rage inside me. It was hard for me to keep my chin up and maintain my pride. In my own home I was queen, but here I felt like a child. . . . Yet, I also knew I had to be careful now. If I complained or found fault, Mrs. Pierce would tell me to get out and find another place. But where could I go with no money. Being so helpless in this place made me feel angry and desperate."

After seven months in the home she still felt the indignity of being treated like a child; yet this lady had effected some positive changes. She located a record player and some records. She encouraged the other residents to take daily walks. They had poetry sessions and a few concerts. After all, these were a far cry from "putting yarn whiskers on sponge rubber mice."

At the end of a year she says, "Almost a year has passed. Is this it? There seems to be nothing else I can do. I've become less rebellious. Maybe there is a need to calm down and be tamed. It takes so much energy to penetrate and be heard. I feel choked;

I can't express myself, and I could contribute so much. As long as this is my home, I want to feel a part of it in some way.

"The music in the parlor is beautiful. We love it. The monotony has lessened. We talk and the music plays softly. Maybe there will be more than pincushions."[3]

And more than pincushions there must be if older persons are to respect themselves. Psychiatrist William Glasser writes in his book *Reality Therapy:*

> Much of what we call senility or senile psychosis is nothing more than the reaction of aged people to isolation. They may be physically near many people but no one is any longer involved with them. A beautifully written example is the play *The Silver Whistle* in which a ne'er-do-well disguises himself as an old man to get into what he thinks is the warmth and comfort of an old folks home. Here he finds the occupants unnecessarily decrepit and senile. By helping them to become involved with each other he restores them to functioning much better than they had dreamed possible. Having had a similar experience working with a ninety-five-year-old patient, I can testify to the almost miraculous effect of getting a very old man involved in life again after he had thought it impossible. From a weak, bedridden, senile man he became a vigorous, self-sufficient, active member of the sanitarium patient group, all in a period of a little over three months.[4]

Glasser's method was effective because involvement with people in a positive way raises a person's feeling of self-worth. One of the great causes of anger in the aged is a very low sense of self-worth.

Whether in a retirement home or living independently, older people can foster relationships which will militate against the anger of isolation. I have never yet seen a patient over sixty who did not have to be pushed hard in this direction. Some seem to have given up on life. They appear to live expectantly waiting for death. They give away their belongings and hole up in their houses. Naturally they are angry, for they have committed themselves to an isolation as strong and binding as any institution.

In contrast some find meaning by doing volunteer work for youth organizations. Some befriend other lonely people, invite them for tea, talk to them on the phone. Many teenagers I know talk to their grandparents because "they understand better." And maybe they do understand, for youth and age have something in common. Youth has not yet found its purpose, and age has passed beyond its peak of functioning. From opposite ends of the spectrum, they understand each other.

Whatever the cause and circumstance, the elderly have a special problem of anger. Understanding that and realizing that we too shall be old some day should help us who are younger help older people more effectively.

Remember, Christ does not condemn anger.

For the Christian the problem of *feeling* anger should never be spiritualized. The mother who feels anger at her son's low grades at school is not sinful nor does that anger have to be confessed as sin. The young man unjustly or even justly released from his job does not sin when he feels anger. Anger is a natural reaction to pain. What we *do* with that anger, however, may have profound spiritual implications.

At one point in my life when everything was seeming to go wrong I suddenly turned to a friend and made some rather cutting, sarcastic remarks. Since it was so contrary to the way I usually handle things, not only she but I was extremely surprised. As we talked I realized three things: my feelings of anger were not sinful, they were normal; my lashing at my friend was wrong and required an apology; my real anger was at God and needed not so much to be confessed as to be relinquished to Him. All I could really say was, "God, I'm angry because I'm hurt but you may take the anger from me." It was a hard prayer because I wanted to hang onto that anger and that was the point at which the problem became spiritual as well as psychological, not before.

Feelings of anger are not pleasant, and held on to they can be a self-destructive force. The challenge before us, therefore, no longer emerges as a need never to feel anger, but rather how to prevent its poison from damaging us and, better still, how to use it as creatively and positively as possible.

NOTES

1. Paul Tournier, *Guilt and Grace* (New York: Harper & Row, 1962), p. 70.

2. Thomas Paine, "The Crisis, No. 1," *American Heritage*, ed. Leon Howard, Louis B. Wright, and Carl Brode (Boston: D. C. Heath and Co., 1955), 1:247.

3. Elizabeth Z. Hughes, "Angry in Retirement," *Human Behavior*, September 1974, pp. 56–59.

4. William Glasser, *Reality Therapy* (New York: Harper & Row, 1965), p. 8.